EASTERN WISDOM

INCLUDES

What is Zen? • *What is Tao?*
A Introduction to Meditation

———————

A L A N   W A T T S

An Introduction to Meditation
has also been published as *Still the Mind.*

MJF BOOKS
NEW YORK

Published by MJF Books
Fine Communications
Two Lincoln Square
60 West 66th Street
New York, NY 10023

Eastern Wisdom
LCCN 2001091577
ISBN 1-56731-491-0

Editors: Mark Watts, Marc Allen
Text Design: Tona Pearce Myers
Interior Calligraphy: Alan Watts

This edition published by arrangement with New World Library

WHAT IS ZEN?

ALAN WATTS

*"Each one of you
is perfect as you are.
And you all could use
a little bit of improvement."*

— Suzuki Roshi, founder
San Francisco Zen Center

CONTENTS

INTRODUCTION

By Mark Watts

Zen is a method of rediscovering the experience of being alive. It originated in India and China, and has come to the West by way of Japan, and although it is a form of Mahayana Buddhism, it is not a religion in the usual sense of the word. The aim of Zen is to bring about a transformation of consciousness, and to awaken us from the dream world of our endless thoughts so that we experience life as it is in the present moment.

Zen cannot really be taught, but it can be transmitted through sessions of contemplation or meditation, called *zazen*, and through dialogues between student and teacher, called *sanzen*. In the dialogue between the student and Zen master the student comes squarely up against the obstacles to his or her understanding and, without making the answer obvious, the master points a finger toward the way.

Zen has enjoyed an increasing popularity in Western literature. D.T. Suzuki's book *Outlines of Mahayana Buddhism* was first published in the English language in 1907, and authors R. H. Blythe, Christmas Humphries, and Alan Watts all made early contributions to Zen literature in the West. Alan Watts wrote his first booklet on Zen in 1933, followed by his first book, *The Spirit of Zen*, in 1936 at the age of twenty-one. He moved from London to New York in 1938, and after spending nearly ten years in the Anglican Church headed west to California in 1950, where he began to teach Eastern thought at the American Academy of Asian Studies in San Francisco.

There he met Japanese artist Sabro Hasegawa and beat poets Gary Snyder and Allen Ginsburg. His classroom lectures spilled over into the local coffeehouses, and in 1953 he began weekly live radio talks on Pacifica station KPFA in Berkeley, California. Early radio series included "The Great Books of Asia" and "Way Beyond the West," which were later rebroadcast on KPFK in Los Angeles. In 1955 he began work on *The Way of Zen* with the help of a Bollingen grant arranged by Joseph Campbell, and following publication in 1957 he went to New York on the first of many cross-country speaking tours that continued over the next fifteen years.

The selections for *What Is Zen?* were drawn from his later talks, given after he had studied and practiced Zen for many years. Most of the material is from recordings made during weekend seminars in which Watts reconsidered Zen with a small group aboard his waterfront home, the ferryboat SS *Vallejo*, in Sausalito, California.

Instead of focusing on the historical background of Zen, he presented the subject directly, in a way he felt would be most accessible to his primarily Western audience. The result is a unique and effective example of the *sanzen* dialogue in practice, and although the words were delivered to a group, the individual's psychological hurdles are addressed with uncanny sensitivity to the "mind traps" that typically confound students of Zen.

In a delightful play of words, Watts's experienced presentation gives us a healthy, heaping serving of the essential wisdom one discovers with the experience of Zen, and points a finger towards the way.

PREFACE

By Alan Watts

Although not long ago the word *Zen* was unknown to most Europeans and Americans, it has for many centuries been one of the most potent influences in molding the cultures of Japan and China. It would be as great a mistake to leave out the consideration of Zen in a history of Japan as to omit Christianity in a history of England.

Zen remained relatively unknown to the world, however, because until rather recently the exponents of Zen were hesitant to spread the doctrine abroad for fear its essence would be lost. This is because Zen is a practice based entirely upon a certain kind of personal experience, and no complete idea of its truths can be given in words. Finally in the early years of the twentieth century various Far Eastern writers — among them the noted Dr. D.T. Suzuki — made known the details of this remarkable way of life. It then became apparent to Westerners that Zen is responsible for many of the things that fascinate us about the Far East, including the martial arts of *judo* and *aikido* and the exquisite aesthetic flavor that characterizes Chinese and Japanese art.

Many hold Zen to be at one with the root of all religions, for it is a way of liberation that centers around the things that are basic to all mysticism: awakening to the unity or oneness of life, and the inward — as opposed to outward — existence of God. In this context the word God can be misleading because, as will be seen, the idea of a deity in the Western religious sense is foreign to Zen.

The aim of this book is to act as a guide to give the contemporary reader some idea of the basic principles of Zen. My intention is to point out the way by offering the rudiments of the path to those whose search for truth has been hindered by the dogmas, creeds, and misunderstood rituals that choke the road of modern religion.

In the Western world we have become accustomed to thinking of spiritual concerns as being distinct from everyday life. We think of the spiritual as being other worldly, and therefore those art forms that portray spiritual subjects do so with symbols of the divine that transcend everyday materiality.

But in the art of Chinese Zen Buddhism one finds a supreme concentration on the most common aspects of everyday life. Even when the great sages of Buddhism are depicted, they are rendered in a secular style, just like very ordinary people, and more often than not as wandering idiots and tramps. The significance of this extremely human portrayal is that it shows us that their attitude about the relationship of the soul to the body and of mind to matter is entirely different from ours — in fact they do not really consider the spiritual life in those categories at all.

We feel that our soul is separate from the body,

that spirit is separate from matter, and by extension that God is separate from the world. And as we
have confronted and tried to reconcile ourselves to
this material world we have come to identify ourselves as a kind of detached soul, and therefore we
have come to feel that there is a problem with material existence. We believe that life is something that
we must conquer, or something we must somehow
get out of. But either way we feel distinct from it,
and think of ourselves not as a part of the natural
material world, but as separate from it, dominating
it, and trying to master it.

The art forms of Chinese Buddhism, however,
express quite a different point of view, a point of
view for which the material, everyday, ordinary
world is not a problem to be solved or a conquest to
be made.

It would be a bit of relief for us if we could see
the world as an extension of ourselves, and ourselves as an extension of the world. In order to
understand how Zen came upon this view one
must consider the environment in which Zen first
arose, which was the native Chinese world of

Taoism. When Buddhism first came to China it was most natural for the Chinese to speak about it in terms of Taoist philosophy, because they both share a view of life as a flowing process in which the mind and consciousness of man is inextricably involved. It is not as if there is a fixed screen of consciousness over which our experience flows and leaves a record. It is that the field of consciousness itself is part of the flowing process, and therefore the mind of man is not a separate entity observing the process from outside, but is integrally involved with it.

As a result, in this philosophy the fundamental conflict between the mind of man and the flow of life is seen to be an illusion, something unreal that we have imagined. This illusion arises because the human memory is a part of this flowing pattern that has the ability to represent former states of the pattern, and this gives the impression of a certain permanence to the behavior of the pattern. We must be aware, however, that our impression of permanence is a kind of thought process that appears to be separate from the pattern upon which the record is written, but is really part of the pattern as well.

The practice of Zen is to experience the overall pattern directly, and to know one's self as the essence of the pattern.

PART I

A SIMPLE WAY,
A DIFFICULT WAY

A Simple Way,
A Difficult Way

Zen is really extraordinarily simple as long as one doesn't try to be cute about it or beat around the bush! Zen is simply the sensation and the clear understanding that, to put it in Zen terms, there are "ten thousand formations; one suchness." Or you might say, "The ten thousand things that are everything are of one suchness." That is to say that there is behind the multiplicity of events and creatures in this universe simply one energy — and it appears as *you*, and *everything* is it. The practice of Zen is to understand that one energy so as to "feel it in your bones."

Yet Zen has nothing to say about *what* that energy is, and of course this gives the impression in the minds of Westerners that it is a kind of "blind energy." We assume this because the only other alternative that we can imagine in terms of our traditions is that it must be something like God — some sort of cosmic ego, an almost personal intelligent being. But in the Buddhist view, that would be as far off the mark as thinking of it as blind energy. The reason they use the word "suchness" is to leave the whole question open, and absolutely free from definition. It is "such." It is what it is.

The nature of this energy is that it is unformulated, although it is not formless in the sense of some sort of "goo" which is just a featureless mess. It simply means that at the *basis* of everything, there is something that never could be made an *object*, and discerned, figured out, or explained. In the same way, our eyes have no apparent color to us as we look at things, and no form of their own. If they had a form of their own, that form would distort all the forms we see — and in some sense their very structure does distort what we see. If the eyes had a color of their own it would affect everything we see, and still we would never become aware of it. As it is, however, we are not aware of the color of the eye, or of the lens, because if it has a color to it that color is basic to all sight. And so in exactly the same way, you might never become aware of the structure and the nature of the basic energy of the world because *you are it*, and in fact, everything is it.

But you might say, "Well, it really doesn't make any difference then." And that is true, it doesn't — but it *does* make a difference in the life and feeling of a person who realizes that that is so! Although it may not make any particular difference to anything that happens, it points directly to the crux of the matter. If there were no eye, there would be no sight, and this tells us something important about our role in the world. We see this sight and that sight, and the structure of the eye does not make any difference from this sight and that, but upon it depends the possibility of seeing. And so upon this energy depends the very possibility of there being a universe at all, and that is rather important.

It is so important, however, that we usually overlook it. It does not enter into our practical considerations and prognostications, and that is why modern logicians in their respective philosophy departments will argue that all assertions about this energy, including the assertion that it is there at all, are meaningless. And that in a way is true, because the world itself is — from the point of view of strict logic — quite meaningless in the sense that it is not a sign or a symbol pointing to something else. But while that is all taken for granted, it nevertheless makes a great deal of difference to how you *feel* about this world, and therefore, to how you act. If you *know* that there is just this; and that it is you; and that it is beyond time, beyond space, beyond definition; and that if you clearly come to a realization that this is how things are, it gives you a certain "bounce." You can enter into life with abandon, with a freedom from your basic fears that you would not ordinarily have.

You of course can become quite "hooked" on the form of life that you are now living. I can consider myself as "Alan Watts" to be an *immensely* important event — and one I wish to preserve and continue as long as possible! But the truth of the matter is that I know I won't be able to, and that everything falls apart in the end. But if you realize this fundamental energy, then you know you have the prospect of appearing again in innumerable forms, all of which in due course will seem just as important as this one you have now, and perhaps just as problematic too.

This is not something to be believed in, however, because if you believe that this is so upon hearsay, then you have missed the point. You really have no need to believe in this, and you don't need to formulate it, or to hang on to it in any way, because on the one hand you cannot get away from it, and on the other hand you — that is, you in the limited sense — will not be there to experience it. So there is no need to believe in it, and if you do believe in it that simply indicates that you have some doubts in the matter!

That is why Zen has been called the "religion of no religion." You don't need, as it were, to cling to *yourself.* Faith in yourself is not "holding on" to yourself, but letting go. And that is why, when a Zen master hears from a student the statement, "Ten thousand formations, one suchness," the Zen master says, "Get rid of it."

That is also why, in the practice of certain forms of Zen meditation, there is at times a rugged struggle of the person to get beyond *all* formulation whatsoever, and to throw away all hang-ups. Therefore the person endures long hours of sitting with aching knees in perpetual frustration to try to get hold of what all this is about. With tremendous earnestness they say, "I have to find out what the mystery of life is to see who I am and what this energy is."

And so you go again and again to the Zen master, but he knocks down every formulation that you bring to him, because you don't need one. The ordinary person, however, upon hearing that you don't need one, will forget all about it and go on and think about something else, and so they never cross the barrier, and never realize the simplicity and the joy of it all.

But when you do see it, it is totally obvious that there is just one energy, and that consciousness and unconsciousness, being and not-being, life and death are its polarities. It is always undulating in this way: Now you see it, now you don't — now it's here, now it isn't. Because that "on" and "off" *is* the energy, and we wouldn't know what the energy was unless it was vibrating. The only way to vibrate is to go "on" and "off," and so we have life and death, and that's the way it is from our perspective.

That is what Zen is about. And that is all it is about.

Of course, other things derive from that, but in Zen training, the first thing to do is to get the *feeling* of its complete obviousness.

Then what follows from that is the question, "How does a person who feels that way live in this world? What do you do about other people who *don't* see that that's so? What do you do about conducting yourself in this world?"

This is the difficult part of Zen training. There is at first the breakthrough — which involves certain difficulties — but thereafter follows the whole process of learning compassion and tact and skill. As Jesus put it, it is "to be wise as serpents and gentle as doves" — and that is really what takes most of the time.

You might then divide the training in Zen into two stages that correspond to the two great schools of Buddhism: the *Hinayana* stage and the *Mahayana* stage. The Hinayana stage is to get to *nirvana* — to get to "living in the Great Void." But then the Mahayana stage is to "come back," as the Bodhisattva comes back from nirvana out of compassion for all sentient beings to help even the grass to become enlightened. And it's that Mahayana aspect of Zen that occupies most of the time of learning to be proficient in Zen.

I offer this by way of introduction just to make everything clear from the start, and to begin without being deceptive about it or befuddling you with cryptic Zen stories! Although the stories are really quite clear, the point often does not come across very easily to Westerners. The fascinating principle underlying Zen stories with all their seemingly irrelevant remarks is quite simple. It is all explained in the *Sutra of the Sixth Patriarch*, when Hui-neng says,

> *If somebody asks you a question about matters sacred, always answer in terms of matters profane. If they ask you about ultimate reality, answer in terms of everyday life. If they ask you about everyday life, answer in terms of ultimate reality.*

Here's an example: Someone says, "Master, please hand me the knife," and he hands them the knife, blade first. "Please give me the other end," he says. And the master replies, "What would you do with the other end?" This is answering an everyday matter in terms of the metaphysical.

When the question is, "Master, what is the fundamental principle of Buddhism?" then he replies, "There is enough breeze in this fan to keep me cool." That is answering the metaphysical in terms of the everyday, and that is, more or less, the principle Zen works on. The mundane and the sacred are one and the same.

PART II

ZEN
RECONSIDERED

ZEN RECONSIDERED

Why study Zen? The first reason that occurs to me is that it is extremely interesting. Since child-hood I have been fascinated by the mystery of being, and it has always struck me as absolutely marvelous that this universe in which we live is here at all. And just out of sheer wonder I have become interested in all of the various answers that people have given as to why all of this is here.

In this sense my approach to religion is not so much that of the moralist as of the scientist. A physi-cist may have a well-developed and highly concrete experimental approach to nature, but a good physi-cist is not necessarily an improved man or woman in the sense of being morally superior. Physicists know certain things, and their knowledge is power, but that does not automatically improve them as people. And the power they have may be used for good or for evil.

But indeed, they do have power, and they have gained that power through their knowledge. I have always thought that in many ways Zen is like Western science; Zen has been used for healing people's sicknesses, but it has also been used by the samurai for chopping off people's heads!

I am interested in Zen for what it reveals about the way the universe is, the way nature is, and what this world is doing. My interest is part and parcel of a greater inquiry, which boils down to this: If you read the literature of the great religions, time and time again you come across descriptions of what is usually referred to as "spiritual experience." You will find that in all the various traditions this modality of spiritual experience seems to be the same, whether it occurs in the Christian West, the Islamic Middle East, the Hindu world of Asia, or the Buddhist world. In each culture, it is quite definitely the same experience, and it is characterized by the transcendence of individuality and by a sensation of being one with the total energy of the universe.

This experience has always fascinated me, and I have been interested in the psychological dynamics of it: why it happens, what happens, and how it comes to be described in different symbols with different languages. I wanted to see if I could discover the means of bringing this kind of experience about, because I have often felt that the traditional ways of cultivating it are analogous perhaps to medieval medicine. There a concoction is prepared consisting of roasted toads, rope from the gallows, henbane, mandrake, a boiled red dog, and all manner of such things, and a great brew is made! I assume that someone in the old folk tradition from which these recipes came understood the potencies of the brew, and that this thing really did do some good. But a modern biochemist would take a look at that mixture and say, "Well, it may have done some good, but what was the essential ingredient?"

In the same way, I ask this question when

people sit in Zen meditation, practice yoga, or practice the bhakti way of religious devotion. What is the essential ingredient? In fact I ask this question of all the various things people do, even when they take psychedelic chemicals. No matter what methods people choose, it is interesting to look at what element these methods share in common. If we eliminate the nonsense and the nostalgia that go with people's attachment to a particular cultural approach, what is left?

It has always struck me as a student of these things that Zen has come very close to the essentials. At least this was my first impression, partly because of the way D.T. Suzuki presented Zen. It seemed to me to be the "direct way," the sudden way of seeing right through into one's nature — *right now*, at this moment. There is a good deal of talk about that realization in Zen circles, and in some ways it is more talk than practice. I remember a dinner once with Hasegawa, when somebody asked him, "How long does it take to obtain our understanding of Zen?"

He said, "It may take you three minutes; it may take you thirty years. And," he said, "I mean that."

It is that *three minutes* that tantalizes people! We in the West want instant results, and one of the difficulties of instant results is that they are sometimes of poor quality. I often describe instant coffee as a punishment for people who are in too much of a hurry to make real coffee! There is something to be said against being in a hurry.

There are two sides to this question, and it strikes me in this way: It's not a matter of time at all. The people who think it ought to take a long time are of one school of thought, and the people who want it quickly are of another, and they are both wrong. The transformation of consciousness is not a question of how much time you put into it, as if it were all added up on some sort of quantitative scale, and you got rewarded according to the amount of effort you put into it. Nor is there a way of avoiding the effort just because you happen to be lazy, or because you say, "I want it now!"

The point is, rather, something like this: If you try to get it either by an instant method because you are lazy or by a long-term method because you are rigorous, you'll discover that you can't get it *either* way. The only thing that your effort — or absence of effort — can teach you is that your effort doesn't work.

The answer is found in the middle way — and Buddhism is called the Middle Way — but it is not just some sort of compromise. Instead, "middle" here means instead "above and beyond extremes."

It is put this way in the Bible: "To him that hath shall be given." Or, to put it another way, you can *only* get it when you discover that you don't need it. You can only get it when you *don't* want it. And so instead you ask, "How do I learn *not* to want it, *not* to go after it, either by the long-term method or by the instant method?" But obviously if you ask that, you still are seeking it, and thereby not getting it!

A Zen master says, "If you have a stick, I will give you one. If you have not, I will take it away from you." Of course this is the same idea as "to him that hath shall be given; and from him that hath not, shall be taken away even that which he hath." So we find ourselves in a situation where it seems that all our normal thinking — all the ways we are accustomed to thinking about solving problems — doesn't work. All thinking based on acquisition is rendered obsolete. We have, as it were, to get into a new dimension altogether to approach this question.

A young Zen student I know said to me recently, "If I were asked what is really essential in Zen, it would be *sanzen*." Sanzen is the dialogue between the master and the student, the person-to-person contact. He said rather than *zazen*, or sitting meditation, it is *sanzen* that is the crux of it. It is in the peculiar circumstances of that dialog that we can get into the frame of mind I am talking about.

In effect this dialog acts as a mirror to one's own mind, because the teacher always throws back to the student the question he's asked! He really does not answer any questions at all, he merely tosses them back at you, so that you yourself will ask *why* you are asking it, and why you are creating the problem the question expresses.

And quickly it becomes apparent that it is up to you. "Who, *me?*" you may ask. *Yes, you!* "Well," you may say, "I can't solve this problem. I don't know how to do it."

But what do you mean by *you*? Who are you, really? Show me the you that cannot answer the question. It is in this kind of back-and-forth dialogue that you begin to understand. Through relationship with the other person you discover that it is you who's mixed up, and that you are asking the wrong questions! In fact, you are trying to solve the wrong problem altogether.

There is a curious thing about gurus — including Zen masters: you notice how people feel that gurus have marvelous eyes, and that they look right through you. And people think, "Oh dear me, they can see to the bottom of my soul. They can read my history, my secret thoughts, my awful misdeeds, and everything. At one glance they know me through and through!"

Such matters are of very little interest to real gurus, however. When they look at you with a funny look, they see who you *really* are, and are looking through your eyes to the divine center.

And here one sees Buddha, Brahma, or whatever you want to call it, pretending not to be at home! It's no wonder the guru has a funny look — they are beholding the incongruity between the divine being that looks out through you in your eyes, and the expression of puzzlement on your face! And so what the guru is going to do in the dialog is to "kid" you out of this irresponsibility — this playing that you are someone other than who you really are. And this, you see, is of the essence.

Don't mistake me, however: I am not saying in order to get there you have to have a guru, and have to go and find one somewhere. That, too, is to go back into the ordinary dimension, back into a state of inner irresponsibility. It is important to realize that *you* give the gurus their authority to do what they do. It is you who says, "be my teacher" — and in Zen they make it very tough for you to get a teacher at all. The Hindus do likewise, and they have various ways of explaining that gurus have to take on the karma of their students, and that is a dangerous thing to do because they become responsible for their students. But this is really just a ploy to force the students to take greater responsibility for their choice in selecting a guru. In Zen they make this process very diffi-cult in the theory that, if you are going to make a fool of yourself by projecting authority onto a guru, you might as well make a *big* fool of yourself. There is no compromise about this!

The point then is this: insofar as you accord spiritual authority to someone, you must recognize that you do it on your own authority. It was you who set this person up as your master. Now you may say, "Well, there were a lot of other people who have done it too, and they can't all be wrong!" And these people form a kind of community, and that gives the appearance of authority to this.

You may want to study with the best Zen master, but who is the best master, and how do you know? If you go around asking people, you are invariably asking the Zen cliché. When you ask someone, "Who do you think is the best master?" you find that people tend to recommend their own teacher, and when a teacher has enough people apply, then they receive great collective authority.

So if you accept that, and say, "I'll go study Zen here," do you see what is happening? You have made the decision to use this group as a pretext upon which to project your own authority without realizing that *you* have done it!

You set the whole thing up, and then the task of the teacher is to show you just what you did. But it all came from you. As the Buddhists say, "All this world is in your own mind."

In the *Tibetan Book of the Dead*, when the instructions are given as to what happens when someone leaves their body after death, it says something like, "When the clear light of the void comes, it is followed by the vision of the blissful Bodhisattvas; then comes the vision of the wrathful Bodhisattvas," and so on. And then it says, "Realize, oh nobly born, that all this is but the outpouring of your own mind."

We don't accept this very easily, however, because we've been most assiduously taught that we are but "little things" in this world. You must be humble, after all, you did not create this world, somebody *else* made it. So watch your "p's" and "q's," and do not for one minute have the spiritual pride of thinking that you are the cause of it all!

And you may very well ask, "How could I have made all this? I certainly don't know how it was made!" But a Zen poem says,

If you want to ask where the flowers come from,
even the God of Spring doesn't know.

There is no way of defining the creative energy of the universe. Suppose God could come and talk to you, and you said, "God, this is a pretty complicated universe — in fact, it is amazing! How did you do it?" And God would say, "I don't know, I just did it."

Of course God does not know — if God had to think out every detail of it, it never would have happened. In just the same way, you breathe and you live: You don't know how you do it, but you are still doing it!

We have been taught by social convention, though, to restrict the concept of "myself" to "what I do voluntarily and consciously." This is a very narrow view of the self. Certainly if you say, "I, by my ego and my intelligence, created all this," you would be conceited, and you know you are a liar. But *you* is much deeper than that; *you* includes far more than your conscious mind. It is the *total you* that not only is responsible for the infinitely complex structure of your physical organism, but also for the environment in which you find yourself. *You* runs that deep.

It is you in that sense, the *total you*, that is the root and ground of everything. And yet we arrange our image of who we are around a principle of human sociability, which is measured by our ability to get along together according to our system of social convention. And as a result we so often end up putting everyone down, including ourselves, because nobody's perfect, and because, as my mother used to say to me, "You're not the only pebble on the beach!"

Why don't we instead try the other technique, and put everyone "up" instead of down? It might be that everyone would get along far better that way than they do by putting everybody down! Of course, whatever you do, you have to do it uniformly for everyone. You can't say, "Well, Johnny is the Lord God, but Peter isn't!"

As a result of our social conventions, we all feel ourselves to be strangers in the world. We are disconnected from it all, and it is something that "happens" to us that we endure passively, and that we *receive* passively. And we never get to the point where we realize we are actually doing the whole thing! It is up to *you*. You make your troubles, and you put yourself into a trap. You confuse yourself, and forget that you did it, and then ask how to get out of it! A verse from the *Mumonkan*, a famous book of *koans*, puts it this way: "Asking where Buddha is, is like hiding loot in your pocket and declaring yourself innocent!"

To finally admit it, and to come to the recognition that it was you, requires a certain kind of nerve. I don't mean "nerve" in the sense of being brash and cheeky. I mean the sort of sense that you use when, for the first time, you take a plane off the ground, or when you pull a cloth off the table and leave all the dishes on the table! *That* sort of nerve has nothing to do with pride in the ordinary sense. It is being ready to leap in, somehow. You see it, and jump in.

But most of us lack that kind of sense. Instead we have what I would call an ambivalent sense of responsibility. We say, "Now, look: It is only me here — just little me. I have certain responsibilities, and they are such and so, but that means as well that there are a lot of things I am certainly not responsible for." And in our social conventions we play games about where we are going to draw the line that defines what we are — and what we're not — responsible for.

When someone is in some kind of social or psychological difficulty, and someone has been irresponsible in some way, we wonder what caused the problem: "*Why* are they like that?" And instead of attributing the problem to the person, our psychologists tend to refer it back to other things and other people: It was because of their environment, or because of family conditioning, or because of their father and mother. But there is no end to that, because you can take the blame straight back to

Adam and Eve! And responsibility is evaded, because it was limited in the first place.

We think that the world is limited and explained by its past. We tend to think that what happened in the past determines what is going to happen next, and we do not see that it is exactly the other way around! What is always the source of the world is the *present*; the past doesn't explain a thing. The past trails behind the present like the wake of a ship, and eventually disappears.

Now you would say that obviously when you see a ship crossing the ocean with the wake trailing behind it that the *ship* is the cause of the wake. But if you get into the state of mind that believes in causality as we do, you see that the *wake* is the cause of the ship! And that is surely making the tail wag the dog!

The point is this: You will never find the mystery of the creation of the world in the past. It never was created in the past. Because truly there *is* nothing else — and never was anything else — except the present! There never will be anything else except the present.

Life is always present, and the past is a kind of echo, a tracing within the present of what the present did before. We can say, "Oh well, we can guess what the present will do next because of what it has done in the past." And this is true: Because of what it does habitually, you may guess it will go on doing it like that. But still it is not the past that controls the present any more than the wake controls the ship. Now from the record of the past you can study the nature of the present and predict what sort of things it's likely to do. But sometimes it surprises you when something new happens, as every so often it does.

It is always in the immediate here and now that things begin. And so, one of the essentials of Zen training is, to quote a certain parrot from Huxley's *Island*, "Here and now, boys!" *Be here.*

And in order to be here, you can't be looking for a result! People keep asking me, "Why do you do this? What do you want to get out of it?" But these questions imply that my motivation is different from my action. It is talking about it in terms of Newtonian billiards — in Newton's explanation of mechanics and behavior he used an analogy with billiards. The balls — the fundamental atoms — are banging each other about; a ball will be still until something bangs it, and that bang will be its motivation, and set it in motion. So when we say, "Human beings behave in such-and-such a way because of unconscious mental mechanisms," this is really Newtonian psychology, and it is out-of-date. Today we need a psychology that is current with quantum theory at least, not one that is tied to mechanical causality.

It is difficult for us to understand this, however, unless we turn things around, as in the analogy of the ship and the wake. If you understand fully that it is from the present that everything happens, then the only place for you to be, the only place for you to live, is here, right now.

People immediately say, however, "Now wait a minute. That's all very well, but I want to be sure that under such-and-such circumstances and in such-and-such eventualities I will be able to deal with it. It's all very well to live in the present when I am sitting comfortably in a warm room reading this, or meditating, but what am I going to do if all hell breaks loose? What if there's an earthquake, or if I get sick, or my best friends get sick, or some catastrophe happens? How will I deal with that? Don't I have to prepare myself to deal with those things? Shouldn't I get into some sort of psychological training, so that when disasters come I won't be thrown?"

That, you would ordinarily think, is the way to proceed — but it doesn't work very well. It is much better to say, "sufficient unto the day is the trouble thereof," and to trust yourself to react appropriately when the catastrophe happens. Whatever happens, you'll probably have to improvise, and failure of nerve is really failure to trust yourself. You have a great endowment of brain, muscle, sensitivity, intelligence — trust it to react to circumstances as they arise.

Zen deals with this. Studying Zen will change the way you react to circumstances as they arise. Wait and see how you deal with whatever circumstances come your way, because the you that will deal with them will not be simply your conscious intelligence or conscious attention. In that moment it will be *all* of you, and that is beyond the control of the will, because the will is only a fragment having certain limited functions.

But if you really know how to live from your center, you live *now*, and know that *now* is the origin of everything. This way, you stand a much better chance of being able to deal with the unforeseen than if you keep worrying about it and considering past lessons and future possibilities.

I know that this sounds impractical to some of you, or perhaps revolutionary, or perhaps not even possible, but it is simply living in the present. It requires a certain kind of poise: If you make exact plans to deal with the future and things don't happen at all as you expected, you are apt to become thoroughly disappointed and disoriented. But if your plans are flexible and adaptable, and if you're *here* when things happen, you always stay balanced.

As in movement or martial arts, keep your center of gravity between your feet, and don't cross your feet, because the moment you do you are off balance. Stay always in the center position, and stay always *here*. Then it doesn't matter which direction the attack comes from; it doesn't matter what happens at all.

If you expect something to come in a certain way, you position yourself to get ready for it. If it comes another way, by the time you reposition your energy, it is too late. So stay in the center, and you will be ready to move in any direction.

This is the real meaning of the practice of *zazen*, or sitting Zen: to sit in the center. As you begin sitting meditation the first thing to do is to find your center, and become comfortable with it, so that you are neither leaning forward nor sitting back. When one's body is balanced in this way the forces of high and low, the heart and breath, and mind and feeling merge at the center.

To sit in zazen in order to perfect a technique for attaining enlightenment, however, is fundamentally a mistaken approach. Sit just to sit. And why not sit? You have to sit sometime, and so you may as well *really* sit, and be altogether here. Otherwise the mind wanders away from the matter at hand,

and away from the present. Even to think through the implications of the present is to avoid the present moment completely.

When you are meditating, it is perfectly fine to be aware of anything that's around: things on the floor, the smell of the atmosphere, the little noises going on. Be there! But when you hear a dog bark, and that starts off a train of thought about dogs in general, about your dog, or somebody else's dog, then you have wandered away from being *here*. Of course you finally will come to the point where you realize there is no way of wandering away from being here, because there is nowhere else to be. Even if you think about somewhere else, past or future, this is all happening *now*.

Through this you will also come to understand how to be a scholar and a historian, if you wish to, and still live in the present. That was how D.T. Suzuki was able to be scholarly and intellectual, and yet at the same time not to depart at all from the spirit of Zen, which is beyond the intellect. You can intellectualize in a Zen way, just as you can sweep floors in a Zen way, but of course the key to the matter is centering — *being really here.* Because this is the point of origin of the world, and it is at the same time the destination of the world.

This is the real meaning of *dhyana,* which in Sanskrit is the kind of concentration or meditation that constitutes Zen. Zen is simply the Japanese way of pronouncing dhyana, and it is that state of centeredness which is here and now.

When you practice zazen, just sit and enjoy yourself being quiet. It is not a duty at all; it is a great pleasure! Get up early in the morning when the sunlight is just beginning to show. It doesn't matter where you are, just sit.

Don't have any thoughts, but don't compulsively try to get rid of thoughts. It's just not important. The real thing is *what is* — what is here, now. After all, here you are, and you may as well see it!

Eventually, a curious feeling will overcome you, one that is very hard to describe in words. I just said that the origin of the world is now — and there is this odd sensation that now comprises everything: the most distant past, the most remote future, the vastness of space, all states of experience, all joy, all sorrow, all heights, all depths. Everything is now. There isn't anywhere else to be — there never was, and never will be!

That is why you never were born, and therefore cannot die. You never came, so you won't go. You were always here. It's a very curious feeling, so different from what we ordinarily think. In entering into the now, we find the *eternal now*. We find infinity in the split second.

As they say in Yoga, liberation lies in the interval between two thoughts. Between the past thought and the future thought lies *now* — there is no present thought.

As one of the Zen texts puts it, "One thought follows another without interruption. But if you allow these thoughts to link up into a chain, you put yourself in bondage."

Actually, this present moment never comes to be and it never ceases to be, it is simply our minds that construct the continuity of thoughts we call time. In the present moment is *nirvana*.

As the great Zen master Dogen explains, in the

course of the seasons, the spring does not "become" the summer. And when wood burns, the wood does not "become" the ashes. There is the state of wood, and then there is the state of ashes. There is the state of spring; there is the state of summer. The spring does not become the summer; the wood does not become ashes; the living body does not become the corpse. That only happens in us, in our minds, when we link our thoughts together. "Oh, no! I will become a corpse!" But you won't. You won't be there when there is a corpse!

If we are going to introduce Westerners to the fundamentals of Zen, we need to revise our understanding of the procedures and rationale of meditation. It should not become a competitive game of one-upmanship, or a marathon to see who can take it, and who can endure. That puts the whole affair right back under the domain of time.

The important thing to emphasize is *presence*, being completely here, and not feeling guilty if you enjoy it. You can do that most easily in any kind of activity that does not require much discursive thought. Anything that you can do without a great deal of thought becomes a perfect form of meditation, whether it's shucking peas, digging up a plot of ground, putting up a fence, or doing dishes.

In Buddhism one hears of "the four dignities of man." It is an extraordinary phrase, when you think about it, especially when you learn the "four dignities" are simply walking, standing, sitting, and lying. Zazen is simply "sitting Zen." There is also "lying Zen," which is sleeping Zen — when you sleep, sleep. There is "standing Zen," and there is "walking Zen." Walking is a very good method of meditation. You simply stroll around, but be right with it! Be *here*.

People have difficulties with these simple forms of meditation. Thoughts and feelings come up: "Is it only this? Is this all there is? Nothing seems to be happening. What's going on? I feel a little frustrated, and I don't particularly feel enlightened. There's just nothing 'special' about this at all. Do I have to do this longer in order for something to happen?"

But nothing special is supposed to happen. It's just *this*. This is it, right here.

You may have difficulty in accepting it because you still feel the lack of nerve to see that *you are all of it*. You are not an observer who is witnessing the present moment as something happening to you. The present that you are experiencing is all of you. It's not "you" here looking at "the floor" there. The floor is just as much you as the organism looking at it. You are doing the floor, just like you're doing your feet. It is all one world — and you're responsible for it.

So enjoy it! Have a good time!

PART III

SPACE

禅

SPACE

Zen represents a simplified way of life. The style and way in which a Zen temple is furnished is completely uncluttered. The rooms of a temple are mostly empty. They are just spaces — but they are *gorgeous* spaces.

Space is the most valuable thing in Japan, and it is treated with great reverence. Here in the United States, where we have so much space, we do not appreciate it. We think that space is equivalent to "nothing," something that simply isn't there. We think of space as a "blank," but in a more crowded situation, people really notice space.

It is interesting that China too is a country

where there is also a lot of space, yet I think it was the Chinese who above all through the arts first taught man to appreciate space. Today we are living in a "space age" and, strangely enough, even though our culture is a pioneer in space navigation and space exploration, we really don't understand the value of space at all. One of the great contributions of Zen to the Western world is understanding space.

The most desirable land for residences in Japan is in the hills. The hills are full of parks and water springs, but the curious thing is that the best land and the most gorgeous sites are occupied by Zen temples. These temples were originally taken away from the brigands, who somehow let the Zen monks come in. These monks essentially put one over on the brigands and occupied the space.

In the Kamakura epoch, Zen had an enormous influence on the samurai warrior caste. This was a time when Japan was torn by internal strife, and constant war was waged between the various feudal lords as they fought to gain control of the imperial power. They went to study Zen as soldiers in order to learn fearlessness — and that was where the Zen monks outfoxed the samurai. The samurai prided themselves on their manly and warrior-like qualities, but they couldn't scare the Zen monks because the monks were just not fazed — not stopped at all — by the idea of death!

A classic Zen story about their fearlessness is the tale of a young man who applied to a fencing master to be his student. The master looked at him and said, "Who did you study with before?"

He said, "I've never studied fencing before."

The master looked at him in a funny way and said, "No, surely, come now, you have studied with someone."

He said, "No sir, I never have studied."

"Well," the master said, "I'm an experienced teacher, and I can tell at once by looking at a person whether he has studied fencing or not. And I know you have!"

But the young man shook his head and said, "Sir, I assure you, I've never studied fencing at all with anybody."

"Well," said the master, "there must be something peculiar about you — what do you suppose it could be?"

"Well," the young man said, "when I was a boy, I was very worried about dying. So I thought a great deal about death. And then I came to the realization that there's nothing in death to be afraid of."

"Oh," said the master, "that explains it."

One of the results of the initial part of Zen training — the beginning of Zen — is overcoming the fear of death. What I described to you earlier as the Hinayana stage of Zen study is where you go deeply into meditation and withdraw your consciousness, as it were, back to its source.

This is the initial stage, and as you go into it, you go down into that dimension of your being where you are deeper than your individuality. And you realize that you belong down here, because this is where you truly exist. What you *feel* as your individuality is really something temporal, like the leaves of a deciduous tree. In the season of the fall, they dry up and drop off.

The Japanese in their poetry and aesthetics always liken death to the fall and winter season. They have a feeling about a human life that is harmonious with the seasons of the year. This theme goes through Japanese poetry, and therefore old people are looked upon as those who are in the "winter" of life, or the "fall" of life. And just as the maple trees in Japan become absolutely gorgeous in the fall, there is an appreciation and a respect for this season of life. Old people in Japan look much better than our old people because they're not fighting with age, they're cooperating with it. It is an honorable thing to be old.

For women and for men, age means respect and authority. This feeling of the harmoniousness of human life with the life cycles of nature makes aging and death less problematic for people with that sort of psychology. They see old age as the proper rhythm of time, not as the deterioration of a living being, just as they don't see the fall and winter as a deterioration of time.

I suppose this may be a difficult correspondence for us to understand, because we simply don't feel the seasons in the same way. So many of us live in a seasonless world.

I mentioned earlier the idea that the great Zen master Dogen put in his book, the *Shobogenzo* — actually, he got the idea from a Chinese student of Kumarajiva, who lived about A.D. 400. Dogen noted that, contrary to appearance, events in time are eternal, and that each event "stays" in its own place. The burning wood does not become ash. First there is wood and then there is ash. The spring does not become the summer. There is spring, then there is summer; then there is fall, then there is winter.

And, curious as it may sound, the sun in its rotation does not move, and the river doesn't flood. It sounds paradoxical to us. It's like the saying from Heraclitus: You never step into the same river twice.

There is a very close parallel between the thinking of Heraclitus and Taoist philosophy; both understand the yang and the yin. Heraclitus is the most original thinker in Western thought. (Phillip Wheelwright published an excellent translation of what remains of the fragments of Heraclitus' philosophy.) If the West had founded itself on Heroclitus rather than Aristotle, we would have been a lot better off, because he was a most ingenious man, and his thought is far closer to Eastern thought.

The Japanese feel that death is a completely natural event; it is only, as it were, the dropping of the leaves, and yet the root underneath is always there. This is difficult for most people to appreciate; the root doesn't seem to enter into our ordinary lives at all. "I feel that I'm only 'on top' — how do I 'get down'?" Well of course the *top* is the top and it can't get down and be the *bottom!*

This is the same question people raise when they ask, "How do I get rid of my egocentricity?" Well, obviously, you can't get rid of egocentricity with your egocentricity — as the master Bankei said, "You can't wash off blood with blood!" And *trying* to realize your Buddha-nature by some sort of egocentric effort is like trying to wash off your ego with your ego, and blood with blood.

In his teaching Bankei emphasized the way in which you have this root in you. He said, "When you hear a bell ringing, you don't have to think about it — you know at once that it's a bell. When you hear the crow cawing, you don't by any effort or cleverness of your conscious will know that it's a crow — your mind does that for you."

Once Bankei was being heckled by a Nichiren priest — those Nichirens can be very fanatical. The Nichiren priest was standing on the fringe of a crowd listening to Bankei, and he called out, "I don't understand a single word you're saying!"

And Bankei said, "Come closer, and I'll explain it to you."

So the priest walked into the crowd, and Bankei said, "Come on, come closer."

And he came closer. "Come closer still!" And he came closer. "Please, closer still" — until he was right next to Bankei. And Bankei said, "How well you understand me!"

Bankei emphasized that we have what he called the "unborn mind" in us, the level of mind that doesn't arise, that isn't born into individuality. We all have that original endowment. When somebody says "good morning," we say "good morning," and we don't "think" to do this — that's the unborn mind. It's the unborn mind through which your eyes are blue or brown; it's the unborn mind by which you see and breathe.

Breathing is important in the practice of meditation because it is the faculty in us that is simultaneously voluntary and involuntary. You can feel that you are breathing, and equally you can feel that it is breathing you. So it is a sort of bridge between the voluntary world and the involuntary world — a place where they are one.

Through focusing on our breathing, and by understanding this concept, we can acquire the sense that our unconscious life is not unconscious at all, in the sense that it lacks consciousness; instead, it is the root of consciousness, the source from which consciousness comes. Just as the leaves

come every year on the tree, so consciousness perpetually comes and goes out of the unconscious
base, or what we could call the *supra*-conscious
base.

In order to appreciate this, you don't need to
believe literally in reincarnation — the idea that
you have an individual, enduring center or soul that
is born into existence time after time after time.
Zen practitioners are divided as to whether they
think this is so or not. I've met masters who believe
in reincarnation, and I've met masters who don't
believe in it at all.

When they talk of the continual reappearance of
individuality and consciousness out of the base,
what they mean is simply something all of us can
see: We see human beings in all stages of life coming
and going. We don't see any continuity between
them.

But that is only because we don't see *space*. It is
the interval between people — the space between
lives — that constitutes the bond between them.
This is very important — the philosophy of space
— and we will get into it in more depth, but the

point here is that through realizing this, those Zen monks had enormous nerve. They could look a samurai in the face and say, "Okay, cut my head off! What does it prove?"

The samurai were amazed by this, and regarded those monks as sort of magical people. They asked the monks to teach them, because they felt if they had that kind of fearlessness, they could never be defeated by an enemy.

Zen is like a spring coming out of a mountain. It doesn't flow out in order to quench the thirst of a traveler, but if the travelers want to help themselves to it, that's fine. It's up to you what you do with the water; the spring's job is just to flow. Zen masters will teach anyone who has the tenacity to go after it, whoever they are. The samurai became grateful students of the Zen monks, and let them occupy the best land in town!

On that land they built buildings that are essentially great, heavy roofs in the Tang Dynasty Chinese style supported by a kind of elegant flimsiness underneath. They're like lanterns — under the roof, empty floors are covered with straw mats; there are sliding screens, and occasional cushions to sit on, and *nothing* else. You get a feeling of "living" space inside.

Let's consider that a moment. I said earlier that in the West we disregard space. We know space here on the planet is full of air, and we know that is "something." Air occupies space and is very important to us, essential to life in fact, but we think of air as simply filling a "void." When astronomers start to talk about curved space, or properties of space, the average person feels that their common sense has been offended. "How could space be curved? How could it have any properties? It isn't there. It's nothing!"

But the folly of thinking that way becomes apparent the moment you realize that solidness, materiality, or density is inconceivable apart from space. Space is the interval between solids, and thus in some sense is the relationship between them.

To understand this, consider for a moment another kind of space altogether: "musical" space

— the interval between notes in a melody. When you play a sequence of notes in a melody, there is no pause, no silence between one note and another; they follow each other immediately. But it is only because of the interval — something that is not stated, *not* "sounded" — that you hear a melody. If you don't hear the interval, you don't hear the melody. The space between the notes, the step, the interval is an essential element in melody. In exactly the same way, it is space — be it interior space or interstellar space — that goes hand in hand with there being any solids or stars. Space isn't just "noth-ing," it is the other pole of something.

Let's look at it from another point of view. We have looked at space astronomically, and musically; let's look at it for a moment aesthetically. In a motel room, for example, when you see the typical "Western" flower print — for some reason or other hotels and motels love flower or bird prints in frames over the bed — you see a bunch of flowers set directly in the middle of a piece of paper. This shows that the person who designed the print has no conception of space, because the space in that print serves merely as background, and is nothing more. It has no function whatsoever; the space is not part of the picture.

When Chinese painters use space, however, you see that if they paint a spray of grass or bamboo or a pine tree, they never set it directly in the middle of the paper. It is set off to one side, so that the object painted is, as we say, "balanced" by the space, and the space is an essential part of the painting. By putting the spray of bamboo to one side, you immediately see the part of the painting that hasn't been touched as *something* — as mist, or even water. The painter doesn't have to do a thing to it — somehow it is all in the picture. The bamboo is not merely set against the background — everything right out to the edge of the piece of paper has been included in the piece by doing this. The artist sees the polarity of space and solid, and uses this polarity in the painting by balancing them against each other.

But you do not feel that balance if the solid area — the painted subject, whatever it may be — is put smack in the middle of the space. Instead, you abolish the importance of the space; it has no "place" in the painting. When we think of a solid object simply sitting in the middle of a canvas, we ignore space.

I have had great fun when visiting college communities by doing experiments in Gestalt psychology that illustrate figure and ground. The Gestalt theory of perception is that we tend to notice the figure and ignore the background. We tend to notice a moving object and ignore what is relatively still. We tend to notice areas that are tightly enclosed rather than those that are diffused.

I draw a circle on the blackboard and say to the group, "What have I drawn?" They inevitably say, "A circle, a ball, a ring," or something like that. And I say then, "Why didn't anybody suggest that I have drawn a wall with a *hole* in it?" It shows us that we tend to ignore the background and pay attention to the figure.

Western artists almost inevitably paint the entire background, because they don't realize that "empty" space is important.

Architects, however, will talk about the "properties" of a space, because they know that what they're doing is making *living* spaces for people. They are enclosing space, and so space has a certain reality to the architect. But to the ordinary person, space just isn't there! We're not aware of it.

It's very interesting that in meditation experiments you can experience various kinds of space: optical space, auditory space, and tactile space. By closing your eyes for a while, you can realize what a blind man's conception of space would be. Every sense has its own appreciation of space.

There was a time in our own history when we can see, by reading between the lines of ancient literature — as late as Dante — that they regarded "space" and "mind" as the same thing. And if you think about it, you can see it is rather obvious. Take the "mind of the eye" — what Buddhists call the *vijnana* — which corresponds to seeing. The basis of sight is a sort of screen, and just as you have a screen on which to project a slide or a movie, there is a kind of ground or area in which everything that is seen must be. You have what we call a "field of vision," which is an oval, with fuzzy edges. You "see" an oval area, this field of vision. There has to be that open field for there to be any vision at all and, though we ignore it, it is the background.

There was once an Englishman and an Indian sitting in a garden together, and the Hindu was trying to explain basic Indian philosophy to the Englishman. So he said, "Look now, there is a hedge at the end of the garden — against what do you see the hedge?"

The Englishman said, "Against the hills."

"And what do you see the hills against?"

He said, "Against the sky."

"And what do you see the sky against?" And the Englishman didn't know what to say.

So the Hindu said, "You see it against consciousness."

In the same way, the space for "being" itself — for material vibration — is the space that we think of as existing between bodies. That is the ground

— the field — which quanta must have in order to play. In the same way that space itself is invisible, consciousness is unknown, because it is not an object of our knowledge. This dimension of your being is like space. This basis is called *amala vijnana* in Buddhist teachings, and it means "without taint." You can't make a mark on space!

The Buddha said, "The path of the enlightened ones leaves no track — it is like the path of birds in the sky."

The Buddhists describe the ultimate reality of the world as *shunyata*, which is often translated as "emptiness" or "the void," or even "the plenum void," meaning it is void, but full of all possibilities. The basic doctrine of Buddhist Mahayana philosophy is given in the *Heart Sutra*:

Form is emptiness; emptiness is form.

To indicate this idea in Chinese, they use a character for *shunyata* or emptiness that also means "sky" and "space." Space is contrasted with the word for form (which also means "shape" and "color"), and the character between them means something like "exactly is" — *space exactly is, or is precisely the same as form*. And when the characters are reversed it says form is precisely emptiness.

The Chinese word for "is," however, is not quite the same as the English or European "is" (in Latin *est*); it means rather "is inseparable from," or "always goes with." The two are interdependent. You can't have space without form; you can't have form without space. They are relational, and in that sense, they *are* each other, because underneath every inseparable relation is a common ground.

To perceive that form reveals the void, and to see that the void reveals form, is the secret for the overcoming of death. To the extent that one is unaware of space, one is unaware of one's own eternity — it's the same thing!

People sometimes imagine that to be aware of the eternal dimension, the forms must disappear. This belief is held by many in India who believe that in *nirvikalpa samadhi*, which is the highest state of consciousness (*samadhi* means the meditation state; concentration; absorption into ultimate reality beyond words; *nirvikalpa* means without concept), is without "content." They will say that in the state of *nirvikalpa* the mind is completely devoid of *any form or motion* whatsoever.

That sounds like a total "blank." And in Zen it is said that a person whose mind is in that state is a "stone" Buddha, just like the Buddha made of stone sitting on the altar: there is no consciousness. There's no point in that, and so in Zen they interpret all this in a very different way indeed. To have *nirvikalpa samadhi*, the highest state of consciousness, is not to have consciousness in which there are no forms, it is simply to reawaken to the *reality* of space. To see that forms come and go in space as the leaves come and go on the trees, as the stars come and go in the sky.

The sky is in a way the mother of the stars, and of course no woman is a mother until she has a child. So in this sense space does not come into being as the matrix of the world until there is something there to nurture. That's why the Chinese use the term "to arise mutually" to indicate the relationship between all opposites: they come into being, they arise mutually.

Space and form arise mutually — as do being and non-being. Then you can see what it means in practical life: To the degree that you are unaware of space, you are unaware of the fullness of your nature.

As our population increases, and we become more crowded, space will become more valuable, and this will help us to be more aware of it. Perhaps that's the reason why species multiply: as *many-ness* increases, the consciousness of *one-ness* increases.

So in Zen, in answer to the question, "What is the ultimate reality?" the master says, "Three pounds of flax."

He chooses something very particular, extremely concrete and "everyday" — something quite worldly — to answer this metaphysical question. Why? Because space does not obliterate the particular, but rather it is precisely the particular, ordinary everyday event that proclaims and advertises the underlying unity of the world.

The many advertise the one — the solid implies and indeed exhibits and brings out the fact that there is space. Were there no solids, there would be no space. If you try to imagine space with no solids, you have to get rid of *yourself* looking at it, because you're a solid in the middle of the space! Space, space, space forever — with nothing in it — is absolutely meaningless, an unimaginable concept. You have to have space and solid — they always go together.

This explains some of the many ways in which Zen life has feeling for space. Here's another very different thing to consider: their idea of poverty. The poverty of the monk, for example, is not poverty as we have thought of it in the Western tradition. It is not poverty as a sort of oppression, where the poor are deprived and feel denuded by poverty. In Zen, poverty is voluntary, and considered not really as poverty so much as simplicity, freedom, unclutteredness.

They have the same feeling for it as they do for purity. The "pure" mind — the "taintless" mind —

means not that you are a "prude," in any sense, because they don't think of purity in that sense at all. It does not mean not having any appetites — not feeling hungry, never feeling sexual, or any-thing like that! In Zen, purity means "clarity." A "pure" eye is a clear eye — without dust in it, just as a pure mirror is a mirror without dust. But the real prototype of purity in Buddhist literature is not so much the mirror as *space* itself. That is purity, clarity, transparency; it is also freedom.

Purity and poverty are simply an absence of pain.

The peculiarly noticeable thing about the per-sonality of Zen people is the uncluttered mind. When you deal with Zen masters, you have a strange feeling that so long as you are with them and addressing them, they are absolutely *with* you. They have nothing else to do but to talk to you. They are just "right there."

They're willing to have some "small talk." They're not like those terribly serious spiritual people who have no time for small talk at all and who can't just pass the time of day! But on the other hand they don't waste time. They don't dither around, and they're never distracted. When something is finished, it's *finished*; and they go right on to the next thing.

You can see this in the way they walk. They have a characteristic walk that is quite different from other Japanese people's walk. This may be partly due to dress, because Zen monks have a wide skirt on their robes, and they stride as they walk, with a kind of a rhythm that is completely characteristic. A Zen monk walking down the street is exactly like a cat crossing the road. When you see a cat crossing the road, the cat always looks as if it knows exactly where it's going. Both cats and Zen monks move in a way that conveys a feeling of freedom.

I stayed one time in an inn on the edge of Nanzengi in the northern corner of Kyoto. I got up early, as I usually do, and sat on the balcony. In the distance I heard this sound: *"Hoa! Hoa! Hoa!"* It came nearer and nearer; then I saw these monks with their big mushroom hats on and their begging bowls held out in front of them. *Hoa* means "the dharma."

They came down the street with a swinging, rhythmic walk: boom-boom-boom-boom-boom! I thought I'd put something in their bowls, and I shot downstairs. But by the time I got there, they were gone.

We had dinner in the monastery that night and I told the priest who was entertaining us about this incident, and said, "You know, I don't think your monks are *serious* about begging! In the early morning the little cart comes with groceries, and it stays around long enough for the housewives to come out and buy their vegetables. At night, there comes a man who sells ramen (noodle soup) on a little cart, and he stays around long enough for people to come out. But your monks don't stay around long enough for anybody to give them anything! I don't think they're really begging at all; they're just fat and rich and their begging is a gesture!"

The next morning I went down early, and stood on the lower level. The monks came by, but they weren't begging at all. They carried their big mushroom hats in their hands in front of them, pointing outwards — the way they hold them when they're just walking, and not begging. There were about three of them walking single-file, Indian style, and the lead monk looked at me and bowed with a kind of evil grin! The priest must have told them what I had said, and their answer was wordless — and comical.

It's so interesting the way they have this "free" walk. You have a sense that, as D.T. Suzuki put it, "a Zen monk is a concentration of energy which is available immediately for anything." In one Zen master's writings, this is likened to water in a vessel. If you make a hole in the vessel, the water immediately comes out. It doesn't stop to think about it.

When you clap your hands, the sound is the clapping of the hands. It comes out at once. It doesn't stop to think. When you strike a stone with steel, the sparks fly immediately!

In the same way, as you can see so clearly in the walk of those who practice Zen, there is always availability, always readiness to act. Therefore they live a life which is empty and spacious — in the sense of being "unblocked." To get rid of blocks is to have space in one's life, the same space we've been talking about all along.

The *heart* doctrine of Buddhism, and the final feeling about the universe at the end of the line, when you *really* get down to it, is called in Japanese *ji-ji-muge*. Or in Chinese, *cher cher mu-gai*. Between all things and events in the universe — *muge* — there is no block. In other words, every thing, every event in the universe that ever happens, *implies all the others*.

And the connection between them is:

space.

Which is no block.

If you can see that space is an effective reality, then you can understand the life and death relationship, because you don't need any more information about this relationship than you already have.

When we watch sparrows, this year's sparrows seem to be the same as last year's sparrows coming back again, because we don't pay much attention to the unique individuality of each particular sparrow.

This is in a way like the story of the fisherman who was using worms for bait. Someone came up to him while he was fishing and said, "It's a terribly cruel thing. How can you put those poor little worms on hooks?" And he replied, "Oh, they are used to it."

We look at our own lives from a perspective in which we are enormously preoccupied with the uniqueness of each life. Somebody else at another level of magnification might see human lives as a vast continuity of comings and goings, and they would be just as right from their vantage point as we are from ours — for after all, all these human beings are just different ways of repeating the same event. Whether you call someone Jane or Joan, or John or Peter, it is always the same person coming back with slight variations — there always have to be slight variations because no two things are quite the same. As is said in Pali, the language of the Buddhist texts, "Each incarnation is not the same, yet not another."

Think about what happens when you die. What will it be like to go to sleep and never wake up? You can't even think about what it would be like because you have nothing to compare it to. It isn't like being shut in the dark forever or buried alive. It is like everything you remember before you were born — after all, what happened once can always happen again.

You know very well that after you die, and after everyone else that you have ever known has died, babies of all kinds — human, animal, and vegetable — will be born. And each one of them will feel that it is "I" in the same way as you do, and each will experience itself to be the center of the universe, exactly as you do. And in this sense, then, each one of them is you, for this situation can only be experienced one at a time.

So you will die, and then someone else will be born, but it will feel exactly as you do now. It will be, in other words, "I" — and there is only one "I," although it is infinitely varied. So you don't have to worry; you are not going to sit and wait out eternity in a dark room.

To put this another way, allow me to make two propositions. After I die I will be reborn as another baby, but I will have no memory of my past life. That is proposition number one. Proposition two is simply that after I die another baby will be born. I maintain that these propositions really are the same thing, because if there is no memory of having lived before then effectively that baby *is* someone else. But after a while you have accumulated so many experiences and collected so many memories that they are lined up like a shelf of mystery stories that you have already read, and it comes time to get rid of them.

You want a surprise, a new situation. You do not want to know what the outcome will be. One of the rules of the game of chess is that if you know the outcome of a game for certain, you cancel it and begin a new one in which the outcome is not certain. This is also part of nature, and so we have to have forgetfulness as well as a memory, just as we have to have a capacity to retain food — the stomach and so on — but also a capacity to reject it. We have to have a hole at each end, and so it is with memory.

By being able to lose yourself utterly — everything you have clung to, everything you have built up, all of your accomplishments and your pride — the world may begin anew, and see itself again through your eyes.

PART IV

ZEN MIND

Zen Mind

If we say that Zen is a certain kind of under-standing of the world, or a certain kind of awareness of the world, we must ask, what kind of awareness is it? It is very often said that Zen lies beyond the intel-lect and beyond logic, and that this kind of under-standing is not accessible to reasoning or any other intellectual processes.

What exactly does this mean? From some points of view, this way of putting it is misleading, because when we say "intellectualizing" and the Japanese say "intellectualizing," we don't necessarily mean the same thing. When in India they say, "The knowledge of Vedanta is not to be obtained from books," this statement has a very specific meaning. It means the books are only lecture notes, and they have to be explained by a teacher.

In the *Yoga Sutra* of Patanjali, the first verse says, "Now yoga is explained." Period. Then the second verse follows. The teachers using these texts know this is just to remind them what to say, in the same way that musical notation for the East Indians is not something you read while you play, it is just to remind you of the basic form of the melody.

The word "now" indicates that something had to go before this; there had to be a preparation before you got to this point in your study of yoga. The word "now" gives the teachers a clue for their pitch.

In the same way, the *Upanishads* in their compact style are simply the notes to accompany the teaching. This is especially true of the *Brahma Sutras*; if you come across Radhakrishna's translation of the *Brahma Sutras* you will find these funny little laconic verses from the sutra, and then pages upon pages of Radhakrishna's commentary. That's one reason why it is said that you can't get it from books.

Another reason is that books by their very nature are intellectual, and the understanding of Zen is intuitive.

What is the difference between intellectual understanding and intuitive understanding? When you talk about these deep matters, people often say, "I understand what you're saying intellectually, but I don't really *feel* it." And I often say, "Well, I don't think you understand it intellectually, because the intellect and the feelings aren't really two different compartments of the mind."

Carl Jung has a schema of the mind as having four functions — intellect, feeling, intuition, and sensation — but these are only colors in a spectrum, as it were. The spectrum of light is continuous, and red is not in a different compartment from blue. Light is all one spectrum, with many colors.

In the same way, we have one mind, and it has various different ways of functioning.

A psychologist was ribbing me a while ago, kidding that I was only proficient in words. "You put on a great talk, but you don't understand it other-wise," he said.

"Don't you put down words like that!" I said, "Words are noises in the air; they are patterns of thought, patterns of intellect, like a fern. Do you put down a fern because it has a complicated pattern?"

"No," he said. "But the fern is real — it's a living, natural thing."

And I said, "So are words! I'll make patterns in the air with words, and make all sorts of concepts and string them together, and they're going to be great! So don't put it down — it's a form of life like any other form of life."

Zen indeed has an intellectual aspect. This aspect is known in Japanese as *kegon*, and in Chinese, *hua-yen*. Hua means the flower, so this is the school of the flower garland.

In Sanskrit, it is what is called *ganda-vyuha*, the most sophisticated form of Mahayana philosophy. When we were talking earlier about *ji-ji-muge*, the mutual interpenetration of all things and events, this is the philosophy that evolved in this school.

The study of yoga has an intellectual aspect, as well. There are various forms of yoga: *bhakti yoga*, which is devotional, emotional, related to feelings; *karma yoga*, which is practical and active; *hatha yoga*, which is physical; and *jnana yoga*, which is intellectual.

But so many people have great difficulty in seeing the bridge between intellectual understanding and intuitive understanding. They know the words, but don't get any real "sense" of the meaning in a way that their sense-experience has changed. When we say "an intuitive understanding," the word "intuition" is subtle, even vague, but "Zen understanding" is sensuous. It is something that you feel not so much in an emotional way as in a direct way, just like when you feel that something is *hard*. As they say, "It is like tasting water and knowing for yourself that it's *cold*." It is sensation, an actual, *physical* sensation.

But how is the intellect related to physical sensation? Or is it completely unrelated? What difference does it make to your sensation whether you think at dawn that the sun is rising or whether you know that the earth is rotating on its axis and revolving around the sun? Is the sensation of a person who does not know that the earth is revolving on its own axis and going around the sun the same as the sensation of a person who does?

Or let's look at another example. There are certain indigenous people in the world whose number system consists of one, two, three, and many. They do not differentiate after "three." For those people it can never be a "fact" that a table has "four" corners — it has "many" corners. So they wouldn't differentiate between a five-cornered and a six-cornered table because they have no "concept system" to give them the cue.

Take an illustration like this — it is very simple, but all depends on concept:

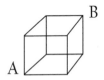

If you have no concept, that drawing is simply a flat-surface pattern. But if it has been explained to you that it is a cube, then you can imagine and actu-ally *sense* the three-dimensionality in it. Now then, let's go further and ask which surface of the cube is in front? Is it the one with corners "A"? Or the one with corners "B"?

You can see it either way, and so you can make either of them the one in "front." Once you've caught on to the idea, it becomes sensation to you — you can actually "feel" it.

This points to the connection between intellect and physical sensation: Concepts lead to sensations — and therefore, false concepts lead to illusions.

We have seen this principle demonstrated before with all kinds of optical illusions. In those illusions our *concept* influences our *sensation*. A cen-tral point in Zen is that we have a concept of our own existence and of the world which is fallacious, and Zen will help us get rid of that concept so that we will have a new sensation. People get worried when they hear this, and say, "Well, are we just going to exchange one hallucination for another?"

Let me respond with a question or two: How do

you know when you know that you know? What is the *test* of "truth" about something that you "feel"?

You may say, "Well, I can feel that I'm Napoleon, or that I'm being persecuted by the government." But this is hallucination — even though one might feel it very strongly.

In our culture, we have a "test" of truth, which is science. We say, "If something can be demonstrated scientifically, then we're inclined to believe that it's not hallucination." All right, let's go along with that. I think this is rather relative, but I will always in any argument grant the premises of the person who wants to argue with me, and take it from there. Let's assume that sciences like biology and physics are ways of discovering the "truth." When we grant that, we find that the hallucination of being a separate ego will not stand up to biological tests!

From the point of view of biology, the individual organism is in the same "behavior system" as the environment, and in fact the organism and the environment constitute a single system of behavior which is neither deterministic nor voluntary. The two are really one activity, and they call it the "field of the organism-environment." Ecology is the study of these kinds of fields.

When I am in academic circles, where people so often think that mystical matters are not at all respectable, I don't talk to them about mystical experience. I talk instead about "ecological awareness." It's just a matter of observing current etiquette and nomenclature, because these are two ways of describing the same reality. From a biological point of view it is perfectly clear that every individual instance of life is a function of the whole universe. This becomes even clearer in quantum theory.

Then you might ask this question: "Why do you scientists — biologists and physicists — who understand this to be so still go on behaving as if you were separate egos?" And they would answer that, in spite of the evidence to the contrary, they still *feel* that way. Their theory is only still at the point of being theory, in that it hasn't convinced them so far as they themselves are concerned. They are still under the social hypnosis that we were all conditioned to in childhood that made us feel as if we are separate egos.

So Zen is a process of "de-hypnotization," if you like. Zen takes away the concepts that are much like optical "tricks," concepts that give us the hallucination of separateness.

Then, when we find out what things are like when the concepts have been taken away, we can say to the biologist, "Isn't this just like you said it was?" And he has to agree. What we arrive at is a state of sensation or feeling that is far more in accord with the findings of science than the ordinary sensation we have of being separate individuals.

So the way in which Zen is non-intellectual is not so much that it regards intellection as something always false and misleading; instead, Zen *begins* by taking away our concepts, and by showing us how to see what it is like to view the world without concepts. Once we have discovered this new view of the world, we can re-fabricate new concepts to try and explain *now* how it is that we see.

For this reason, many Zen masters are also great intellectuals. In the history of Zen there have been scholars of all kinds, and physicists in modern times. Zen does not rule out the life of the intellect. It only says, "Do not be hoaxed by concepts."

Is Zen illogical? Illogical is not the right word, because what often appear in Zen to be paradoxes are statements that make perfect sense in another system of logic than that to which we're accustomed. We in the West are accustomed to a kind of logical thinking that is based on exclusiveness — "either-or." Chinese logic, on the other hand, is based on "both-and."

To us it is either "black" or "white," it either "is" or it "is not," it is either "so" or it is "not so." This kind of logic is fundamental to our thinking, and so we emphasize the mutually exclusive character of logical categories: "Is you is or is you ain't?" Is it in the box or outside the box?

In so many of our tests we are asked "true" or "false," "yes" or "no," and we're given *only* those choices. It's amusing to think that when we toss a coin to decide whether we will do it or we won't, we have only a two-sided coin. The Chinese are able to toss a sixty-four-sided coin by using the *Book of Changes* in the same situations where we would toss a coin. It's a rather nice idea, when you think about it, and even though the *Book of Changes* is based on yin and yang, black or white, you can get everything out of black and white if you provide for all of the permutations that are possible — just as you can get all numbers out of zero and one in the binary system. But whereas we think something is either/or — either black or white — both Indian and Chinese logic recognize that black and white are inseparable, that in fact they *need* each other, and so it isn't a matter of making a choice between them.

"To be or not to be" is *not* the question — because you can't have one without the other! Not-being implies being; just as being implies not-being.

The existentialist in the West — who still trembles at the choice between being and not-being and therefore says that anxiety is ontological — hasn't grasped this point yet. When the existentialist who trembles with anxiety before this choice realizes suddenly one day that not-being implies being, the trembling of anxiety turns into the shaking of laughter.

Nothing has changed except one's perception. And in the same way, you may have the same view of the world — just what you're looking at now, seeing everything that you see now — but it can have a completely different feeling, and a completely different meaning to it. Because in one's ordinary sensation of the world the *differentiations* — the solids — are stressed, and the space is ignored.

But when you practice Zen meditation, you have a kind of a "conceptual alteration," and then suddenly you notice the physical world — everything you're seeing now — in a completely different way. You see that it all goes together; it's all-of-a-piece. You see that every inside implies its outside, and every outside implies its inside.

You may think now, in the ordinary way we're conditioned to think, that "I — me, myself — am *only* on the inside of my skin." But when you experience this perceptive "flip," you discover your outside is as much *you* as your inside. You can't have an inside without an outside, so if the inside is yours, then the outside is yours!

Finally you have to acknowledge that the world *outside* your skin is as much yours as the world inside the skin. And even though everybody's outside appears different to us, in reality everybody's outside is all the same! Do you see?

It is in this way that we're one.

Your soul isn't in your body; your body is in your soul!

That's why the ancients were partly correct with their astrology. When they drew a "map" of a person's soul, they drew a crude map of the universe as it was at the moment of the person's birth, seen from that place and time. That map, that horoscope, is considered to be a "picture" of that person's mind — because your mind is not in your head, your head is in your mind. And your mind is the total system of cosmic interrelationships as they are focused at the point that you call "here and now."

The question is then: Can this become clear to us? Can it become clear in the way a *sensation* is clear, as when we taste water and know for ourselves that it is cold? The experience of this requires some meditation, and it also depends on an intellectual process.

We get *into* trouble through an intellectual process and we're going to get *out of* trouble through an intellectual process. From an intellectual standpoint, the process by which we get into trouble could be called "additive," whereas the process by which we get out of trouble is "subtractive." In the words of Lao-tzu, "The scholar gains every day; the man of Tao loses every day."

The scholar acquires ideas, and in Zen the intellectual operation is to get rid of ideas — to see that *all* ideas are projections that we make upon the cosmic Rorschach blot.

The world is a Rorschach blot, full of movement and wiggles. Only when we see straight lines and grid-iron patterns do we know *people* have been around. People are always trying to straighten things out, and so we create straight lines!

Look at how the stars are sprayed across the heavens. In order to "make sense" of the stars, we can get stellar maps and see straight lines joining the stars in various patterns to make up constellations. But all those joining lines are of course projections by which we try to make sense of the stars.

In the same way we make projections upon the surface of nature for the purpose of discussing it with each other — and, inevitably, some person with a strong will and a powerful and compelling personality describes the world in one way, and everybody else agrees with him. That's the way it is. And it's passed down through the generations.

So now, let's go back to seeing that the world is a primordial Rorschach blot. Wiggles of the world unite; you have nothing to lose but your names!

Once you see the movement and the wiggles to be what they are, once you realize that we have created the world from our own projections, you see then that the difference between your *inside* (your ego, your self) and the *outside* (the subject-perceiver and the object-perceived) is artificial.

You can confirm this realization through neurology, because neurologists will tell you that the so-called "external world" that you see is experienced by you only as a state of your own nervous system. What you see out in front of you is an experience in the nerve ganglia in the back of your head, and you have no other awareness of an external world *except in terms of your own body.*

You can infer that your body is, in turn, something "in" the external world, but you only know it by union with it. You are in the external world, and scientist and mystic alike will tell you that you are an inseparable part of it.

Yet "part" isn't even the right word, because the world doesn't have "parts" like an automobile engine — it isn't bolted or screwed together. The world is like a body: When your body was born, it grew not by the addition of "bits," but by an organic process in which the whole thing constellated itself at once. It grew larger and larger, growing from the inside to the outside.

It did it in a field called the *womb.* And the womb could only do it in a field called a *female body.* And a female body could only do it in a field called *human society,* in a field called *the biosphere of the planet Earth.* If you take the body out of its field, it cannot grow.

Blood in a test tube cannot do what blood in the veins does, because all of the body's conditions have to be replicated, and that's impossible in a test tube, because it's a different environment.

Just as words change their meaning in accordance with the context of the sentence, so organisms change their nature in accordance with the context of their environment. Even from this strictly scientific point of view, our body-mind — contrary to what we usually feel — is not something separated from other minds and from the external world. *It is all one process.* If we don't feel that to be so, it is because we have been indoctrinated with concepts that contradict the facts. The concept of what we might call the "Christian ego" simply does not fit in with the facts of life; it has become a social institution that is obsolete.

When we say "social institution," people usually think of things like hospitals, parliaments, police forces, fire departments, and so forth. But marriage is a social institution, the family is a social institution, the clock and the calendar are social institutions, latitude and longitude are social institutions. And *the ego* is a social institution; it is, in other words, a "convention" (from the Latin *convenire*, "to come together"); it is a consensus, an agreement. With it we are agreeing to a set of rules for the purpose of playing a game.

What happens, however, is that we are apt to confuse the rules of our social game with the laws of nature — with the way things are. Even the "laws of nature" are social conventions. Nature does not obey a lawgiver who says, first of all, this is the way things shall be, and then all beetles, all butterflies, all rocks, and so on follow it. The laws of nature are *our* way of describing what we believe to be "regular behavior" in nature.

But what is regular? Interestingly, *regulus* in Latin means a "rule." And what is a rule? It is a ruler — it is marked-out in inches, it is straight, and you measure things with it. But you don't find rulers growing on trees! Nature is all of a piece, and everything in it goes with everything else in it, in an eternal dance. But we chop it so that we can discuss it and even try to rule it.

Laws of nature are therefore tools, like axes,

hammers, and saws; they are instruments we use to control what is going on. To keep in touch, then, with what is really going on in the present, always preserve this careful distinction between the game rules of the human game, and the behavior of the world in itself. It is true that the behavior of the world in itself includes the human games, and it's all a part of nature. But don't try to make the tail wag the dog.

The whole point of Zen is to suspend the rules we have superimposed on things and to see the world as it is — as all of a piece. This has to be done in a special setting of some kind, because you can't just gaily walk out into the street and suspend the rules. And if you do, you'll create traffic confusion of every conceivable kind!

But we can set up a certain environment in which we have an agreement to suspend the rules — that is to say to meditate, to stop thinking for a while, to stop making formulations.

This means, essentially, to *stop talking to yourself.* That is the meaning of the word in Japanese — *munen*

— that is ordinarily translated as "no thought." To meditate is to stop talking to yourself!

We say, "Talking to yourself is the first sign of madness," but we don't follow our own advice. We're talking to ourselves most of the time — and if you talk all the time you've got nothing else to talk about but your own talking! You never listen to what anybody else has to say, without a running commentary of your own talking. And if all you ever listen to is talking — be it your own or other people's — you have nothing to talk about but talk.

You have to *stop talking* in order to have something to talk about!

In the same way, you have to *stop thinking* in order to have something to think about, because otherwise all you're thinking about is thoughts — and that's *scholarship*, as we practice it in the universities today, where we study and write and talk about books about books about books!

In order to be able to symbolize, to think effectively, one has to suspend thought occasionally and be in a state of what I will call "pure sensation." Drink water, and know for yourself that it's cold. Sit, just to sit.

> *Sitting quietly doing nothing.*
> *Spring comes and the grass grows by itself.*

You can take that literally or you can take it symbolically. But that is the meaning of *munen.*

Sometimes the word used is *mushin* — no mind. *Mushin* means being open to the way that the world is experienced sensuously, without the distortion of concepts, so as to find the original nature before any thought is made.

It is the way you experienced it when you were first born, before you thought any thoughts about it! It is called your original mind, or the "root mind."

One of the koans that are studied in the Rinzai school of Zen is: "Who are you before your father and mother conceived you?" You could put it this way: "Who are you before your father and mother bamboozled you!" Conceived is used in the sense of "thought about" you, or taught you to conceive.

What is your original mind? Before all this started, *where were you really?*

To go back to that, you have to take a fresh look at the world. You have to come to it unprejudiced, with your mind wiped *clean*, like a mirror, of all conceptions about life and what it is.

Even now, of course, I am giving you conceptions about the unity of the world and about the process of meditation. And those who understand these words still have difficulty if they've *only* got the conception. It may alter their feeling to some extent, and their sensation, but not nearly as vividly as their sensation will be altered if they look at the world *without any conception at all.*

"Well," you might say, "how can we stop? We think perpetually — we are always talking to our-selves. It's a nervous habit!"

To stop thinking, there are certain technical aids:

Concentrate on breathing, and think of nothing but your breathing — in and out, in and out.... One, two, three, four, five.... One, two, three, four, five.

Or look at a point of light and think of nothing else but the point of light — just concentrate, concentrate, on that light.

Both of these help you to eliminate all concepts from the mind except that which you are concentrating on. The next thing is to get rid of the point you're concentrating on.

Most people think that means a "blank mind," but it doesn't. You concentrate on something in order to cause the thought process, the verbalizing, to stop. Then when you take away the point of concentration, you are simply perceiving the world *as it is*, without verbalizing.

The trick of concentration stops our verbalizing. Concentration is only preliminary. It leads us deeper, beyond concentration, until we reach the state of *samadhi*. This is *dhyana*, in Sanskrit — which came to be called *c'han* in China and *zen* in Japan. It is not concentration in the ordinary sense, like staring at a point or thinking of one thing only. It comes after concentration has stopped, after the point on which you have concentrated has fallen away, after your body and mind have fallen away, and you're open to the world with your naked senses.

See that.

That is the foundation experience.

After you see that, and on the *basis* of seeing that, you can, of course, go back to concepts and construct this idea of the world, that idea, and the other idea.

This is why Zen does not really involve any beliefs in any theory or doctrine. In this sense, it is *not* religion — if by religion you mean something that involves a system of beliefs. It is purely experimental and empirical in its approach, and it allows us to *get rid of belief* — to get rid of all dependence upon words and ideas.

This is not because words and ideas are "evil," nor because they are *necessarily* confusing; it is just because we do happen to be confused by them at this stage in our evolution.

That is really the essential nature of the whole meditation process: the suspension of talking to yourself, either in words or in any other conceptual image.

It is of interest that words are a form of notation — words are the notation of *life*. Just as musical notation is a way of writing down music so as to remember it, words are essential vehicles of memory: we repeat them, we write them down, and we remember. That gives us a wonderful sense of control, but to the extent that we are tied to our notations, we pay a price for it.

In music, notation limits our ability to conceive of variations and other musical forms. The Hindu, however, is not tied to notes in music, and therefore values a kind of music in which a musical instrument — be it a drum, flute, or sitar — is immediately responsive to every subtle motion of the human organism. They therefore play things —

odd quarter-tones and strange rhythms — which are impossible to reproduce with our notation.

The Hindu rejoices in the extreme subtlety of a flute, so responsive to human breath, an organic phenomenon. When they listen to our music, it all sounds very structured and rigid to them, like a military march, because of the regular beat and the fixed harmonic intervals.

In the same way, when you get free from certain fixed concepts of the way the world is, you find it is far more subtle, and far more miraculous, than you thought it was. You find that human relationships and situations are amazingly subtle. And you gain a facility for understanding them, not through conceptualizing, but through asking your brain how it would deal with them.

Your brain is an organ like your heart, and it can deal with situations without having to think about them! The brain is not only an organ of thought — only one of its functions is thinking. The brain does a lot of things other than thinking, and enables your body and mind to perceive and act in new, unique, and wonderful ways.

You have a fantastic computer in your skull — and what we call "thinking" is only fifteen percent or less of the brain's activity. The brain is very active in controlling all our organic processes — our gland functions, our digestion, our circulation, and everything else. The brain is in control of the entire autonomic nervous system. Through the practice of Zen, you can learn to use your nervous system in a much more wonderful way than you would ever have thought it could be used!

By practicing Zen, you find you can let your nervous system answer questions and pass through problems without any interference from your conscious thinking process. We cannot solve the puzzle of the Zen koans or of the situations we encounter in life through our conscious thinking process — but the brain will! And the practice of Zen shows us how.

WHAT IS TAO?

ALAN WATTS

The tao that can be told
is not the eternal Tao.
The name that can be named
is not the eternal Name.

The unnameable is the eternally real.
Naming is the origin
of all particular things.

Free from desire, you realize the mystery.
Caught in desire, you see
only the manifestations.

CONTENTS

INTRODUCTION

By Mark Watts

The ancient philosophy of the Tao is one of the most intriguing and refreshing ways of liberation to arrive in the West from the Far East in modern times. With over fifty translations of the *Tao Te Ching* into Western languages to date, the classic work of Taoist literature offers its readers great wisdom for living as well as advice on worldly affairs. It is also a fascinating window into the mysterious world of pre-dynastic China.

The very practical nature of Taoist thought is often overlooked by Western readers who are hesitant to embrace a seemingly strange and foreign way of knowing, but in the philosophy of the Tao one finds a surprisingly contemporary perspective. The word *Tao*, properly pronounced "dow," has lent its name to a way of understanding and living in the world with profound implications for modern societies. Above all else Taoism places great emphasis on the balance between our human awareness and our natural being, as an integral part of the web of life. It embodies our deepest understanding of ecological awareness.

The mystical side of Taoist thought, on the other hand, is highly enigmatic, for here one finds a doorway into the shamanistic world that flourished in China over a span of at least five thousand years, right up to the period in which the Taoist texts were written.

As Alan Watts explains it, the word Tao embodies two broad meanings in our language: it means approximately the Way — in the sense of "the way to go" — and it also refers to nature in the sense of one's own true nature. Everything is said to have its own Tao, but it is impossible to define it, to put one's finger on it exactly.

As I sat working on this manuscript my eight-year-old son came up to me and asked, "Papa, what are you working on?" I told him it was a book on the Tao, and began to explain a little bit about it, but without a moment's hesitation he said, "Oh, you mean what's behind everything" — and then he headed off. Intuitively and experientially we know what it is, but for most of us the problem arises when we try to explain it.

This enigma reminds me of a story that my father used to tell about a debate years ago in the House of Lords in England concerning a Church-related matter. Apparently one of the representatives had put forth the argument that it was not proper for a governing body with so many atheists to rule on a religious issue. One of the members rose to the occasion, however, and replied, "Rubbish, Sir! I am quite certain that everyone here believes in some sort of something somewhere or other." And by and large we do even if it is no more definite than to sense the Tao.

In classic Chinese literature the Tao is described as following the path of least resistance, occupying the invisible or lowest position, and embracing the goodness of nature without ever attempting to do so. The Tao is passive but not weak, and in his book the legendary sage Lao-tzu describes the paradoxical quality of the Tao by asking one to consider the following:

How do coves and oceans become kings of the hundred rivers?
Because they are good at keeping low —
That is how they are kings of the hundred rivers.
Nothing in the world is weaker than water,
But it has no better in overcoming the hard.

THE ORIGIN OF THE TAO TE CHING

The *Tao Te Ching* has traditionally been attributed to Lao-tzu, the legendary sage and founder of the Taoist school. However, the *Tao Te Ching* was originally called the *Lao-tzu* as well, and this makes it difficult for us to fully understand the origin of the earliest texts describing its origin because in

Chinese it is often impossible to know whether "Lao-tzu" refers to the person or the text. Nevertheless the original work has been tentatively dated to the sixth century B.C.E., the time in which Lao-tzu was supposed to have lived, although it is likely that the collection did not come into circulation until the fourth century B.C.E. This was the period of the golden age of Chinese philosophy that gave rise to tremendous diversity — known as "the hundred schools" of thought — and gave us the other great classic of Chinese literature, the *I Ching*.

It is not until the first century B.C.E., however, that we find a history, the *Shih chi* (or *Records of the Historian*), that contains one of the oldest recorded stories about Lao-tzu. Here we find the story of Confucius visiting Lao-tzu at the Court of Chou where, by this account, Lao-tzu served as the court librarian. In that meeting, Lao-tzu was said to have scolded Confucius for his pompous and self-serving ways, and afterward Confucius is reported to have said to his disciples:

"I know that birds can fly, fish can swim, and animals run. For those that run a net may be set, for those that swim a line cast, and for those that fly an arrow set free. But a dragon's ascent to heaven walks the wind and swims through clouds, and I know of no way to trap him. Today I have met Lao-tzu, who is both man and dragon."

The reference to the ascension of the dragon to heaven offers a clue to the early origins of Taoist rituals, because it reveals a link to the ancient shamanic ancestry of the region. The dragon, like the Feathered Serpent in South and Central American mythology, combines the scales of the snake with the feathers or wings of the bird. The feathers or wings of the dragon or bird are repre-sentative of the shaman's flight, and the scales rep-resent rebirth, for the snake sheds its skin only to find a new one beneath the old.

The combination of these attributes accurately describes dream/death and rebirth rituals of the shamans known to date far back into the Neolithic period. Pottery dating from 5000 B.C.E. discovered in the village of Banpo near Xi'an in the 1950s included a ritualistic vessel showing four views of a shaman in a dreaming or trance state, and a fifth as a transformed being. This pottery example is fairly typical of representations of the wizards who were said to leave their bodies in flights of vision, and following such a flight the shaman or initiate would be reborn with the sunrise fully trans-formed.

Although the antiquity of the underpinning is apparent, the actual history of the legendary sage Lao-tzu has proved to be elusive. To further obscure matters, the histories we do have that mention Lao-tzu were not recorded until hundreds of years after the events they detail, and it is possible that some of the facts were adapted to corroborate the legendary accounts of the origin of his works.

One popular legend holds that the *Tao Te Ching* was written in the gatehouse by Lao-tzu as he was about to leave his post in the city to retire and become a hermit in the country. According to this story the gatekeeper is said to have insisted that Lao-tzu record his wisdom before he left. Another more plausible theory is that the philosophy was recorded over a period of time by several anony-mous writers to give the benefit of the country dwellers' wisdom to the rulers of the cities, in the hope they would make life easier for the common people — and the gatehouse story may simply be symbolic of the source of this knowledge originating outside the pale. This theory fits in with the tumultuous climate of the Warring States period, and is supported by the fact that the later chapters of the work carry decidedly political overtones and candidly offer advice to those in positions of authority.

In the first century A.D. the *Lao-tzu* was divided into two works, and so we received the *Tao Ching* and the *Te Ching*. This division reflects the varying emphasis of each section of the book, the first on the Tao and the second on *Te*, which means approximately "virtue," though Alan Watts calls it "skill at living." These sections were then combined to form the book we know today.

Some scholars firmly believe the *Tao Te Ching* is in fact a compilation of writings by various authors who simply attributed their works to the legendary Lao-tzu; however, the consistency of the style and the rhythm of the arguments presented in both parts of the work suggest otherwise. It seems more likely that this book of sage advice was the work of a single author drawing upon the prevailing folk wisdom of his day, and that perhaps the two books were written during different periods of the author's life, or in response to different issues.

THE PHILOSOPHY OF NATURE

Taoism has often been described as the philosophy of nature, and it is in this respect that its wisdom most strongly suggests its origins were in the shamanic world of pre-Dynastic China. Living close to the earth one sees the wisdom of not interfering with the course of life, and of letting things go their way. This is the wisdom that also tells us not to get in our own way, and to paddle with the current, split wood along the grain, and seek to understand the inner workings of our nature instead of trying to change it.

According to the laws of nature every creature finds its own way, and so each of us is known to have our own path or way. In classic Chinese texts there are references to the Tao of Earth with all its creatures, the Tao of Man, which refers to our awakened path, and to the Tao of Heaven, by which the broad forces of heaven and earth come together in a field of polar energies. Together these forces create the world in which all life plays, and instill in us the instinctive knowledge of the primal forces at work in the human psyche.

In this book, Alan Watts brings his years of study of the Tao into focus through lively explanations of the essential ideas and terms of Taoist thought. He gives the reader an opportunity to experience the Tao as a personal practice of liberation free from the limitations of the commonly held beliefs within our culture. This book is based on talks given during seminars during the last ten years of his life, and it offers a way of understanding the true value of ourselves as free-willed individuals enfolded within the ever-changing patterns of the natural world.

We explore the wisdom of the way things are of themselves *(tzu-jan,* or "by itself so"), and of letting

life unfold without interference and without forcing matters when the time is not right *(wu wei,* or
"not forcing"). In the philosophy of the Tao we soon
discover that striving to succeed — in the theory
that "you can't get something for nothing" — must
be balanced by the realization that "you can't have
something without nothing," because something
always requires its opposite, a place to be, whether
it is a receptive vessel, a clear mind, or an open
heart.

PART I

THE WAY
OF THE TAO

When people see some things as beautiful,
other things become ugly.
When people see some things as good,
other things become bad.

Being and non-being create each other.
Difficult and easy support each other.
Long and short define each other.
High and low depend on each other.
Before and after follow each other.

Therefore the Master
acts without doing anything
and teaches without saying anything.

Our Place in Nature

Many years ago, when I was only about fourteen years old, I first saw landscape paintings from the Far East. It was as a result of looking at these paintings that I first became interested in Eastern philosophy. What grasped me and excited me about the Asian vision of the world was their astonishing sympathy and feeling for the world of nature.

One painting in particular that I remember was called *Mountain after Rain*. It showed the mist and clouds drifting away after a night of pouring rain, and it somehow pulled me into it and made me feel part of that mountain scene. It is fascinating for us to consider that pictures of this kind are not just what we would describe as landscape paintings, because they are also icons, a kind of religious or philosophical painting.

In the West, when we think of iconographic or religious paintings, we are accustomed to pictures of divine human figures and of angels and saints. When the mind of the Far East expresses its religious feeling, however, it finds appropriate imagery in the objects of nature, and in this very important respect their feeling for nature is different from ours. The contrast in these two forms of expression arises as a result of the sensation that the human being is not someone who stands apart from nature and looks at it from the outside, but instead is an integral part of it. Instead of dominating nature, human beings fit right into it and feel perfectly at home.

In the West our attitude is strangely different, and we constantly use a phrase that sounds peculiar indeed in the ears of a Chinese person: We speak of "the conquest of nature" or "the conquest of space," and of the "conquest" of great mountains like Everest. And one might very well ask us, "What on Earth is the matter with you? Why must you feel as if you are in a fight with your environment all the time? Aren't you grateful to the mountain that it lifted you up as you climbed to the top of it? Aren't you grateful to space that it opens itself up for you so you can travel right through it? Why do you even think of getting into a fight with it?"

Indeed, it is this domineering feeling that underlies the way we use technology. We use the powers of electricity and the strength of steel to carry on a battle with our external world, and instead of trying to live with the curvature of the land we flatten it with bulldozers, and constantly try to beat our surroundings into submission.

The problem is that we have been brought up in a religious and philosophical tradition that, to a great extent, has taught us to mistrust the nature that surrounds us, and to mistrust ourselves as well. We have inherited a doctrine of original sin, which tells us not to be too friendly, and to be very cautious of our own human nature. It has taught us that as reasoning and willing beings we should be suspect of our animal and instinctual nature.

In one sense this is all very well, for we have indeed achieved great technological advances through harnessing the powers of nature. If we carry this effort beyond a certain point, however, our manipulations interfere with the very course of nature, and this gets us into serious trouble indeed.

As a result of our interference we are experiencing today what we could call the "law of diminishing returns." For example, we want to go faster and faster everywhere we go, and so we attempt to obliterate the distance between ourselves and the place we are trying to reach. But as the result of this attempt to minimize the span of the Earth between these points, two things begin to happen.

First, all places that become closer and closer to each other by the use of jet planes tend to become the same place. The faster you can get from Los Angeles to Hawaii, the more Hawaii becomes exactly like Los Angeles. This is why the tourists keep asking, "Has it been spoiled yet?" What they are really asking is, "Is it just like home?"

Second, if we begin to think about our goals in life

as destinations, as points to which we must arrive, this thinking begins to cut out all that makes a point worth having. It is as if instead of giving you a full banana to eat, I gave you just the two tiny ends of the banana — and that would not be, in any sense, a satisfactory meal. But as we fight our environment in our tendency to get rid of the limitations of time and space, and try to make the world a more convenient place to live, this is exactly what happens.

For a much better understanding of our place in nature, we can look to the great religions and philosophies that blossomed and took deep root in the consciousness of so much of the population throughout Asia and the Far East.

Taoism and Confucianism

There are two great main currents in traditional Chinese thinking: the Taoist current and the Confucian. Both of them agree on one fundamental principle, and that is that the natural world in which we live, and human nature itself, must be trusted. They would say of a person who cannot trust his own basic nature, "If you cannot trust your own nature, how can you trust your own mistrusting of it? How do you know that your mistrust is not wrong as well?" If you do not trust your own nature, you become as tangled up as anyone can be.

Their idea of nature is that which happens of itself so, and that is a process which is not fundamentally under our control. By definition it is that which is happening all on its own, just as our breathing is happening all on its own, and just as our heart is beating all on its own — and the fundamental wisdom behind Taoist philosophy is that this "self-so" process is to be trusted.

Taoist thought is generally attributed to Lao-tzu, who is thought to have lived somewhere around 400 B.C.E., and to Chuang-tse, who lived from 369 to 286 B.C.E. Taoism is known to us as the uniquely Chinese way of thought, living, and liberation, although its roots certainly lie in shamanic traditions common to much of northeastern Asia, and probably to North America as well. In its final form, however, it is so similar to Buddhism that Taoist terms are often used to translate Sanskrit texts into Chinese. Once Buddhism was imported to China, Taoism so completely permeated Mahayana Buddhism in general and Zen Buddhism in particular that the philosophies of these schools are often indistinguishable.

Like Vedanta and yoga in India, older gentlemen in China traditionally adopted Taoism after they had made their contribution to society, and thereafter they would retire to primitive dwellings or caves to live in the wild and meditate for long periods of time. As in Buddhist lore, where the return of the sage into the world is known as the path of the Bodhisattva, Taoist stories are filled with accounts of the return of the liberated sage into worldly affairs. In fact the primary text, the *Tao Te Ching*, was originally written as a manual of advice for the ruling class. The teachings of Lao-tzu and of Chuang-tse must not be confused, incidentally, with the Taoist cult of alchemy and magic preoccupied with life extension — that is Taoist only in name, and not in practice.

Although Taoism proper has never become an organized religion, it has attracted the curiosity of scholars and philosophers of the Far East for more than two thousand years.

Taoism regards the entire natural world as the operation of the Tao, a process that defies intellectual comprehension. The experience of the Tao cannot be obtained through any preordained method, although those who seek it often cultivate inner calm through the silent contemplation of nature. Taoists understand the practice of *wu wei*, the attribute of not forcing or grasping, and recognize that human nature — like all nature — is *tzu-jan*, or "of-itself-so."

When we look to Confucian ideas, which governed Chinese moral and social life, we find a different word that represents the basis of human nature. This word has a funny pronunciation, and although we Romanize this word in English as *jen*, it is pronounced "wren," with a sort of rolling "r." This word is symbolic of mankind's cardinal virtue in the system of Confucian morality, and it is usually translated "human-heartedness" or "humanness." When Confucius was asked to give a precise definition of it, though, he refused. He said, "You have to feel the meaning of this virtue. You must never put it into words."

The wisdom of his attitude toward defining *jen* is simply that a human being will always be greater than anything they can say about themselves, and anything they can think about themselves. If we formulate ideas about our own nature, about how our own minds and emotions work, those ideas are always going to be qualitatively inferior — that is to say, far less complicated and far less alive — than the actual author of the ideas themselves, and that is us. So there is something about ourselves that we can never get at, that we can never define — and in just the same way you cannot bite your own teeth, you cannot hear your own ears, and you cannot make your own hand catch hold of itself. So therefore you must let go and trust the goings-on of your humanness. Confucius was the first to say that he would rather trust human passions and instincts than trust human ideas about what is right, for like the Taoists he realized that we have to allow all living things to look after themselves.

THE WORLD AND ITS OPPOSITES

When we say what things are, we always contrast them with something else, and when we try to talk about the whole universe — about all that there is — we find we really have no words for it. It is "one *what?*"

All of this "one what?" is represented by the symbol of the great circle. But in order to think about life, we have to make comparisons, and so we split it in two and derive from the circle the symbol of the yang and the yin, the positive and the negative.

We see this symbol over and over on Chinese pottery, and today on everything from jewelry to T-shirts. Traditionally this emblem is one of the basic symbols of the philosophy of Taoism. It is the symbol of the yang, or the male, and the yin, the female, of the positive and the negative, the yes and the no, the light and the dark. We always have to divide the world into opposites or categories in order to be able to think about it. In the words of Lao-tzu,

> *When people see some things as beautiful,*
> *other things become ugly.*
> *When people see some things as good,*
> *other things become bad.*
>
> *Being and non-being create each other.*
> *Difficult and easy support each other.*
> *Long and short define each other.*
> *High and low depend on each other.*

LAO-TZU

In the literary tradition of Taoism, the legendary Chinese philosopher Lao-tzu is often referred to as a contemporary of Confucius. According to some accounts, Lao-tzu was supposed to have been a court librarian who wearied of the insincerity and intrigue of court life and decided to leave the city and go off and live in the mountains. But before he left, the guardian of the gate is said to have stopped him and said,

"Sir, I cannot let you go until you write down something of your wisdom."

And it is said that he sat down in the guardhouse and recorded the book known as the *Tao Te Ching*, the book of *Tao* and *Te*, of the Way and its power.

The core of Lao-tzu's written philosophy deals with the art of getting out of one's own way, learning how to act without forcing conclusions, and living in skillful harmony with the processes of nature instead of trying to push them around. Lao-tzu didn't actually say very much about the meaning of Tao; instead, he simply offered his advice.

It is now believed that although this work was probably rendered in a single hand during the time of Confucius, or shortly thereafter, the author incorporated the wisdom of a much older folk tradition. One school believes that Taoist literature was inspired by the oral teaching of shamanic hermits in ancient times. Another holds that the *Tao Te Ching* was an attempt to bring the practical, conventional wisdom of the Chinese people to the ruling class in order to help them to rule with greater wisdom and compassion. Both schools are probably partially correct, and in either case Taoist thought remains among the most accessible of the world's great religious philosophies, and is perhaps the only one to retain a sense of humor.

My favorite picture of Lao-tzu is by the master Sengai, and it shows him in the sort of disheveled and informal style that is so characteristic of Taoist humor, and was later assimilated in Zen Buddhism. This playfulness is one of the most delightful characteristics of the whole of Taoist philosophy and, as a result, I know of no other philosophical works besides those of Lao-tzu and his successor Chuang-tse that are so eminently readable. Of all the great sages of the world, they alone have a sense of the enjoyment of life just as it comes.

Lao-tzu literally means "the old fellow," since Lao means "old" and tzu means "fellow," or sometimes boy. So Lao-tzu is the old boy, and he is sometimes shown as a white-bearded youth, which is of course symbolic of his great wisdom at an early age.*

Long before Buddhism came to China in about 60 A.D., Lao-tzu's philosophy had revealed to the Chinese that you cannot characterize reality, or life itself, as either being or non-being, as either form or emptiness, or by any pair of opposites that you might think of. As he said, "When all the world knows goodness to be good, there is already evil."

We do not know what any of these things are except by contrast with their opposite. For example, it is difficult to see a figure unless there is a contrasting

---

*You will find the writings of both Lao-tzu and his contemporary Chuang-tse in a book called *The Wisdom of Lao-tzu*, translated by Lin Yutang. He has arranged the Lao-tzu book that was supposed to have been written for the guardian of the gate, and then added quite a few substantial excerpts from the book of Chuang-tse as a running commentary on Lao-tzu's passages. [Editor's note: That book is currently out of print. There are of course many other editions in print.]

background. Were there no background to the figure, the figure would vanish, which is the principle of camouflage. Because of the inseparability of opposites, therefore, you realize that they always go together, and this hints at some kind of unity that underlies them.

TAO

In Lao-tzu's philosophy this unity is called *Tao*. Although it is written t-a-o, in Chinese it is pronounced almost as if it were spelled d-o-w. It has the sense of a rhythmic motion, of going on and stopping, and also a sense of intelligence, and so you get an idea of a sort of rhythmic intelligence that ebbs and flows like the tides.

The word has two general meanings. One is perhaps

best rendered into English as "the way," "the way of things," or "the way of nature." The other sense of the word means "to speak," so when the opening words of Lao-tzu's book say,

The Tao that can be spoken is not the eternal Tao,

it makes a pun in Chinese. It says literally, "The Tao that can be Tao is not Tao," or if you read it like a telegram, "Tao can Tao no Tao." The first meaning of Tao is "the way," and the second meaning of it is "to speak," or in other words,

The way that can be expressed is not the eternal way.

I prefer not to translate the word Tao at all because to us Tao is a sort of nonsense syllable, indicating the mystery that we can never understand — the unity that underlies the opposites. In our deepest intuition we know that there is some sort of unity underlying these various opposites because we find that we can't separate one from the other. We know that a whole universe exists, but we can't really say what it is. So

Tao is thus a reality that we apprehend deeply without being able to define it.

A Chinese poet put it this way:

> *Plucking chrysanthemums along the eastern fence,*
> *gazing in silence at the southern hills,*
> *the birds fly home in pairs,*
> *through the soft mountain air of dusk.*
> *In all these things there is a deep meaning,*
> *but when we're about to express it,*
> *we suddenly forget the words.*

Lao-tzu also said, "Those who speak, do not know; those who know, do not speak." And another Chinese poet satirized him by saying, "Those who speak, do not know; those who know, do not speak; thus we have heard from Lao-tzu, and yet how does it come that he himself wrote a book of five hundred characters?" The point, then, is that his whole book does not in any way define what the Tao means. He speaks not so much about it, but rather speaks with it, using it, as it were, as the power by which to express himself.

So what is the reason why Tao is inexpressible and yet at the same time the basis for a philosophy? The reason is that we cannot have any system of thought — whether it be philosophical, or logical, or mathematical, or physical — which defines its own basis. This is an extremely important principle to understand. In other words, I can pick up a paint brush with my right hand, but I can't pick up my right hand. My right hand picks itself up. If I try to pick up my hand, what would I pick it up with? There always has to be something, as it were, that isn't picked up, that picks itself up, that works itself and is not worked upon.

In the same way, you will find that if you look up "to be" in a dictionary, it is defined as "to exist." Then when you look up "to exist," you will find it defined as "to be." And are you any the wiser? A dictionary cannot really completely define itself; ultimately it can only put words together that correspond to other words.

In this sense, to try to say anything about the Tao is like trying to eat your own mouth, and of course you cannot get outside of it to eat it. Or to put it the other way, anything you can chew is not your mouth. Anything that is expressed about the Tao is not the Tao.

Tzu-Jan

By Itself So

There is always something that we don't know. This is well illustrated by the elusive qualities of energy in physics: We cannot really define energy, but we can work with it, and this is the case with the Tao. The Tao works by itself. Its nature is to be, as is said in Chinese, *tzu-jan*, that which is "of itself," "by itself," or "itself so." Tzu-jan is almost what we mean when we say that something is automatic, or that something happens automatically. We sometimes translate this expression in English as "nature," as when we talk about the nature of the mountains, the birds, the bees, and the flowers. That sort of nature in Chinese would be tzu-jan.

The fundamental sense of it is that the Tao operates of itself. All that is natural operates of itself, and there is nothing standing over it and making it go on. In the same way one's own body operates of itself. You don't have to decide when and how you're going to beat your heart; it just happens. You don't decide exactly how you are going to breathe; your lungs fill and empty themselves without effort. You don't determine the structure of your own nervous system or of your bones; they grow all by themselves.

So the Tao goes along of itself. And since there is always a basic element of life that cannot be defined — in the same way the Tao cannot be defined — it cannot be controlled. In other words, you can't get outside yourself to define yourself or to control yourself. Lao-tzu would go on to say that since man is an integral part of the natural universe, he cannot hope to control it as if it were an object quite separate from himself. You can't get outside of nature to be the master of nature. Remember that your heart beats "self-so" — and, if you give it a chance, your mind can function "self-so," although most of us are afraid to give it a chance.

Wu Wei

Not Forcing

Whenever we have the feeling of being able to dominate ourselves, master ourselves, or become the lords of nature, what happens is that we do not really succeed in getting outside of nature or of ourselves at all. Instead we have forced our way of seeing these things to conform to an illusion that makes us think they are controlled objects, and in doing this we invariably set up a conflict inside the system. We soon find that the tension between our idea of things and things as they are puts us out of accord with the way of things.

For this reason you might say that *not-forcing* is the second principle of the Tao — the spontaneous or *of-itself-so* activity (tzu-jan) being the first. In Chinese the second principle is called *wu wei*, and it means literally "not doing," but would be much better translated to give it the spirit of "not forcing" or "not obstructing." In reference to the Tao it is the sense that the activity of nature is not self-obstructive. It all works together as a unity and does not, as it were, split apart from itself to do something to itself.

Wu wei is also applied to human activity, and refers to a person who does not get in his or her own way. One does not stand in one's own light while working, and so the way of wu wei (this sounds like a pun but it isn't) is the way of non-obstruction or non-interference. This is the preeminently practical Taoist principle of life.

What I mean by forcing yourself is something like this: When children in school are supposed to be paying attention to the teacher, their thoughts will go wandering all over the place, and the teacher will soon get angry and say, "Pay attention." And the children will wrap their legs around the legs of the chair, and they will stare at the teacher and try to look frightfully intelligent. But what happens was expressed very well in a cartoon I saw the other day: A small boy is standing and looking at his teacher and saying, "I'm sorry, I didn't hear what you were saying because I was listening so hard." In other words, when we try to be loving, or to be virtuous, or to be sincere, we actually think about trying to do it in the same way the child was trying to listen, tightening up his muscles and trying to look intelligent as he thought about paying attention. But he wasn't thinking about what the teacher is saying, and therefore he wasn't really listening at all. This is a perfect example of what is meant by blocking yourself or getting in your own light.

To offer another illustration of it, suppose you are cutting wood. If you go against the way the tree grew, that is to say against the grain of the wood, the wood is very difficult to cut. If you go with the grain, however, it splits easily. Or again, in sawing wood, some people are in a great hurry to get on with sawing and they try and power right through the piece. But what happens? When you turn the board over you see the back edge of the wood is full of splinters, and you find that you are rather tired as well. Any skilled carpenter will tell you, "Let the saw do the work, let the teeth do the cutting." And you find that by going at it quite easily, and just allowing the blade to glide back and forth, the wood is easily cut.

As our own proverb says, "Easy does it." And wu wei means easy does it. Look out for the grain of things, the way of things. Move in accord with it and work is thereby made simple.

TE

Virtue: Skill at Living

In one book the philosopher Chuang-tse tells a wonderful story about a butcher who was able to keep the same chopper for twenty years because he was always careful to let the blade fall on the interstices between the bones. And so in this way he never wore it out.

Once again we see that the person who learns the kind of activity which is, shall we say, in accord with the Tao, is said to possess virtue. This peculiar Chinese sense of virtue is called *Te*, but it is not virtue in quite our ordinary sense of being good. Te is like our word virtue when it is used more in the sense of the healing virtues of a plant. When we use the word virtue in this way it really designates an extraordinary kind of skill at living. And in his book Lao-tzu says the superior kind of virtue is not conscious of itself as virtue, and thus really is virtue. But the inferior kind of virtue is so anxious to be virtuous that it loses its virtue altogether.

We often come upon the kind of virtuous person who is self-consciously virtuous, who has, you might say, too much virtue. These are the sorts of people who are a perpetual challenge to all their friends, and when you are in their presence you feel they are so good that you don't know quite what to say. And so you are always, as it were, sitting on the edge of your chair and feeling a little bit uncomfortable in their presence. In a Taoist way of speaking, this kind of person stinks of virtue, and doesn't really have any virtue at all.

The truly virtuous person is unobtrusive. It is not that they are affectedly modest; instead they are what they are quite naturally. Lao-tzu says that the greatest intelligence appears to be stupidity, the greatest eloquence sounds like a stammer, and the greatest brightness appears as if it were dull. And of course this is a kind of paradoxical way of saying that true virtue, Te, is the living of human life in such a fashion as not to get in its own way.

This is the thing we all admire and envy so much about children. We say that they are naive, that they are unspoiled, that they are artless, and that they are unself-conscious. When you see a little child dancing who has not yet learned to dance before an audience, you can see the child dancing all by itself, and there is a kind of completeness and genuine integrity to their motion.

When the child then sees that parents or teachers are watching, and learns that they may approve or disapprove, the child begins to watch itself while dancing. All at once the dancing becomes stiff, and then becomes artful, or worse, artificial, and the spirit of the child's dance is lost. But if the child happens to go on studying dance, it is only after years and years that, as an accomplished artist, the dancer regains the naivete and the naturalness of their original dance. But when the naturalness is regained it is not just the simple, we could say embryonic, naturalness of the child, completely uncultivated and untutored. Instead it is a new kind of naturalness that takes into itself and carries with itself years and years of technique, know-how, and experience.

In all this you will see that there are three stages. There is first what we might call the natural or the childlike stage of life in which self-consciousness has not yet arisen. Then there comes a middle stage, which we might call one's awkward age, in which one learns to become self-conscious. And finally the two are integrated in the rediscovered innocence of a liberated person.

Of course there is a tremendous advantage in this, because one must ask, if you are enjoying life without knowing that you are enjoying it, are you really enjoying it? And here, of course, consciousness offers an enormous advantage. But there is also a disadvantage, even a danger, in developing it, because as consciousness grows, and as we begin to know how to look at ourselves and beyond ourselves, we may start over and over again, and cause much interference with ourselves. This is when we begin to get in our own light.

You know how it is when you get in your own light or get in your own way — when it becomes desperately essential that you hurry to catch a train or plane, for example, instead of your muscles being relaxed and ready to run, your anxiety about not getting there in time immediately stiffens you up and you start stumbling over everything. It is the same sort of thing on those days when everything goes absolutely wrong. First of all, when you're driving to the office, all the traffic lights are against you. Of course this irritates you, and because of your irritation you become more tense and more uptight in your way of handling things, and this leads to mistakes. It could lead to being so furious and going so fast that the police stop you, and so on and so forth. It is this way of battering against life, as it were, that ties it up in knots.

And so, the secret in Taoism is to get out of one's own way, and to learn that this pushing ourselves, instead of making us more efficient, actually interferes with everything we set about to do.

PART II

THE GENTLE WAY

The Tao is like a well:
used but never used up.
It is like the eternal void:
filled with infinite possibilities....

The Tao is called the Great Mother,
empty yet inexhaustible,
it gives birth to infinite worlds.

It is always present within you.
You can use it any way you want.

The Strength of Weakness

Lao-tzu writes about the philosophy of the strength of weakness. It is a strange thing, I think, how it is men in the West do not realize how much softness is strength. One of old Lao-tzu's favorite analogies was water. He spoke of water as the weakest of all things in the world, and yet there is nothing to be compared with it in overcoming what is hard and strong. You can cut water with a knife and it lets the knife go right through, yet water alone cut the Grand Canyon out of solid rock.

Lao-tzu also said that while being a man, one should retain a certain essential feminine element, and that he who does this will become a channel for the whole world.

The ideal of the hundred-percent tough guy, the rigid, rugged fellow with muscles like steel, is really a model for weakness. We probably assume this sort of tough exterior will work as a hard shell to protect ourselves — but so much of what we fear from the outside gets to us because we fear our own weakness on the inside.

What happens if an engineer builds a completely rigid bridge? If, for example, the Golden Gate Bridge or George Washington Bridge did not sway in the wind, and if they had no give, and no yielding, they would come crashing down. And so you can always be sure that when a man pretends to be 100 percent male on the outside, he is in doubt of his manhood somewhere on the inside. If he can allow himself to be weak, he can allow himself to experience what is really his greatest strength. This is so not only of human beings, but of all living things.

JUDO

The Gentle Way

The philosophy of the strength of weakness that came from China to Japan through the migration of Zen Buddhism has inspired the astonishing forms of self-defense known as judo and akido. The word *judo* is fascinating because it means *ju*, the gentle, *do*, way. *Do* is the Japanese way of pronouncing the Chinese Tao, and so it is the gentle Tao, the philosophy of the Tao as applied to self-defense.

This philosophy has various components, and one of the most basic elements to the whole practice of judo is an understanding of balance — and balance, indeed, is a fundamental idea in Taoist philosophy. The philosophy of the Tao has a basic respect for the balance of nature, and if you are sensitive you don't upset that balance. Instead you try to find out what it is doing, and go along with it.

In other words you avoid such mistakes as the wholesale slaughter of an insect pest or the introduction of rabbits into a country like Australia without thought as to whether they have a natural enemy, because through such interference with the balance of nature you inevitably find yourself in trouble. The philosophy of balance is the first thing that all students of judo and akido have to learn, and it is the underlying principle of the Tao.

If we look at the principles of judo, the question of balance is easily demonstrated by looking at what happens when we try to lift a heavy roll of material. We would be foolish to try and just pick it up from the top, because that shows no under-standing of the laws of balance. If you want to lift something, go below its center of gravity. Put your shoulder to it, undermine it, and then swoop it up. That principle follows throughout judo. Part of the understanding of balance in judo is to learn to walk in such a way that you are never off center: your legs form the base of a triangle, and your body is on the apex, and when you turn you always try to keep your feet approximately under your shoulders, and in this way you are never off balance. This is a good practice in everyday life as well as in judo.

The second principle, beyond understanding and keeping balance, is not to oppose strength with strength. When you are attacked by the enemy, you do not oppose him. Instead you yield to him, just like the matador yields to the bull, and you use his strength and the principle of balance to bring about his downfall.

Suppose, for example, there is a blow coming at me from a certain direction. Instead of defending myself, and pushing the blow off, the idea in judo is to carry the blow away. But as the adversary goes by, the knee goes out, catching him below his point of balance. The adversary then falls heavy and hard — brought about by his own initiative, and your receptivity. By letting him follow his punch through, and not deflecting it, he has fallen into your trap.

The same attitude of relaxed gentleness is most beautifully seen when you watch cats climbing trees. When a cat falls out of a tree, it lets go of itself. The cat becomes completely relaxed, and lands lightly on the ground. But if a cat were about to fall out of a tree and suddenly made up its mind that it didn't want to fall, it would become tense and rigid, and would be just a bag of broken bones upon landing.

In the same way, it is the philosophy of the Tao that we are all falling off a tree, at every moment of our lives. As a matter of fact, the moment we were born we were kicked off a precipice and we are falling, and there is nothing that can stop it. So instead of living in a state of chronic tension, and clinging to all sorts of things that are actually falling with us because the whole world is impermanent, be like a cat. Don't resist it.

Li

The Patterns of Nature

Thus far, like a typical philosopher, I have been trying to explain what Taoism is, and odd as it may seem, this is really quite the wrong thing to do.

Stranger still, if I succeed in giving you some sort of impression that you really understand, if I succeed in making the whole problem clear in words, I shall have deceived you. One reason life seems problematic to us, and one reason why we look to philosophy to try to clear it all up, is that we have been trying to fit the order of the universe to the order of words. And it simply does not work.

Yet I continue to talk and write about Eastern philosophy, and I have often said that the real basis of Buddhism is not a set of ideas but an experience. This of course is equally true of Taoism as well, which like Buddhism recognizes that experience is altogether something different from words. If you have tasted a certain taste, even the taste of water, you know what it is. But to someone who has not tasted it, it can never be explained in words because it goes far beyond words.

The order of the world is very different from the order we create with the rules of our syntax and grammar. The order of the world is extraordinarily complex, while the order of words is relatively simple, and to use the order of words to try to explain life is really as clumsy an operation as trying to drink water with a fork. Our confusion of the order of logic and of words with the order of nature is what makes everything seem so problem-atic to us.

When we say that we are trying to make sense out of life, that means that we are trying to treat the real world as if it were a collection of words. Words are symbols, and they mean something other than signs formed out of letters, but actual people, mountains, rivers, and stars are neither symbols nor signs. And so the difficulty that we encounter in trying to make sense out of life is that we are trying to fit the very complex order of life itself into a very simple system that is not up to the task, and this gets us involved in all sorts of unfore-seen difficulties.

In the Chinese language there are two terms that signify these two different orders. The first is the word *tsu*, which means "the order of things as measured," or "the order of things as written down." In one sense this word has the meaning of "law," and although we sometimes speak of the laws of nature, the laws of nature could never be *tsu* unless we made an attempt to describe them or write them down in order to think about them in words.

Since *tsu* only refers to the order of things as we think about them in words or numbers, the Chinese use another word, *li*, for the actual order of nature. This is a peculiar and interesting term; its original meaning is the markings in jade, the grain in wood, or the fiber in muscle, and it has been translated by the great student of Chinese thought, Joseph Needham, as "organic pattern." It refers to the kind of complex pattern we see when we look at the stars, for example, and see a gaseous nebula, which is an extremely indeterminate form, or when we look at the sculpted layers forming the patterns in a rock, and see the glorious rippling that is incredibly difficult to describe, although easy enough to understand with our eyes and our feelings. But to try to put that kind of order into words is always beyond us, and it is for this reason that the attempt to make sense out of life will always fail.

The order of *li*, of the infinite complexity of organic pattern, is also the order of our own bodies, and of our brains and nervous systems. We actually live by that order, for as I have often noted we do not figure out in words or ordered thoughts how we grow our own bodies, structure our bones, or regulate our metabolism. In fact we really have no idea how we manage to do any of this, no idea how we manage to be conscious, how we actually think, and how we actually make decisions. We do these things, but the processes and the order of the physical body that underlies them are completely mysterious to us. Even though we can do these things, we cannot fully describe them.

All the time we are actually relying on this strange and unintelligible form of natural order. It is at the basis of everything we do, and even when we try to figure something out and describe it in words, and then make a decision on the basis of that process, we are still unconsciously relying upon an order that we cannot figure out. That order constitutes our basic nature, but we are too close to it to see it — and so following the Tao is the art of feeling our way into our own nature.

In the process of our upbringing, however, and particularly in our education, our parents and teachers are very careful to teach us not to rely on our spontaneous abilities. We are taught to figure things out, and our first task is to learn the different names for everything. In this way we learn to treat all of the things of the world as separate objects.

A tree is a tree, and it begins with its roots, and ends with the leaves on its branches, and that's that. We are also taught to behave consistently, almost as if we are characters in a book, and you know how the critics hate an author who doesn't make his characters consistent. If we were actually consistent in life it would be very boring, but I think that sometimes, in this respect, we take our cues for living from literature, and attempt to impose a consistency on top of our natural, ever-changing spontaneity.

Since we are brought up to make sense of ourselves, and to be able to account for ourselves, we are always expected to be able to rationalize our actions in words. When we try to accomplish this we develop a kind of second self inside us, which in Zen is called the observing self. This observing self can be a very good thing for us to develop, and it can also cause problems, and run a commentary on who we are and what we are doing all the time. It asks, "What will other people say? Am I being proper? Does what I am doing make any sense?"

The sociologist George Herbert Meade called this "the interiorized other." That is to say, we have a kind of interior picture, a vague sense of who we are, and of what the reaction of other people to us says about who we are. That reaction is almost invariably communicated to us through what other people say and think, but soon we learn to maintain the commentary on our own, and each thought or observation is then compared to the idea we have formed. Therefore this image becomes interiorized — a second self who is commenting all the time upon what the first one is doing — and in any given situation we must either rationalize why a certain behavior is consistent with that image, or force ourselves to change that behavior, or fail to change it and feel guilty for failing. The difficulty with this is that although it is exceedingly important for all purposes of civilized intercourse and personal relationships to be able to make sense of what we are doing, and of what other people are doing, and to be able to talk about it all in words, this nevertheless warps us.

We have all admired the spontaneity and freshness of children, and it is regrettable that as children are brought up they become more and more self-conscious. In this way people often lose their freshness, and more and more human beings seem to be turned into creatures calculated to get in their own way.

Humans get in their own way because they are always observing and questioning themselves. They are always trying to fit the order of the world into the order of sense, the order of thought and words. And therefore the children lose their naturalness and spontaneity. For this reason we admire the people, whether they be sages or artists, who have the ability to return in their mature life to a kind of childlikeness and freshness. They are not bothered any more by what people are thinking or saying. This is the charm that surrounds the Taoist sages of ancient China.

I Ching

Book of Changes

For an illustration of the pattern intelligence of *li*, and of how it can be used in decision making, let's look at an ancient Chinese method of divination that is infused and linked inextricably with Taoism. Perhaps you know of divination as a kind of fortune-telling, but this particular form of divination is based on what some people believe to be the very oldest of all the Chinese tracts, the *I Ching*, or the *Book of Changes*. As such, I think one would not presume to ask such an ancient and honored book of wisdom as the *I Ching* what to bet on the stock market, but rather one asks questions about one's spiritual or psychological state or consults the oracle concerning momentous decisions in life.

The old and orthodox way of consulting the *Book of Changes* is to use the stalks of a yarrow plant, which are long, straight, and narrow. A number of stalks are taken and divided at random, and then the calculations are made. But this is a rather long and elaborate way of casting, and the not-so-ancient but equally respectable way is to use coins. I keep three Chinese coins for this purpose; any other coins work just as well.

The kind of question to ask the *Book of Changes* that would be appropriate under most circumstances is something like this: "What is the best thing for me in my present state?" We phrase a clear question, and then take the coins and shake them and drop them; according to the way they fall on each toss — heads or tails — we construct a six-line hexagram consisting of a pair of three-line trigrams.

It works like this: We shake and throw all three

coins together at the same time; each throw of the three coins gives us a single line. The inscribed side of the Chinese coin — or the "tails" side of an American coin — counts as yin, with the value of 2. The reverse side — or the "heads" side of an American coin — counts as yang, with a value of 3. There are then four different possibilities for the three coins:

If all the coins are yin, the total value of all three coins is 6, and a broken line, or negative line, is drawn, and forms the bottom line of the hexagram. This is the so-called "old yin" line:

If two coins are yin and one is yang, the total value is 7, and an unbroken, or positive, line is drawn, the so-called "young yang" line:

If one coin is yin and two are yang, the total value is 8, and a broken, or negative, line, the so-called "young yin," is drawn. And if all three coins are yang, the total value is 9, and an unbroken, or positive, line is drawn: the "old yang."

Let's look at a particular case, and assume that on the first throw we get a total of 6, a negative reading, and the symbol that records the negative reading is the drawing of a broken line, a yin line.

We do it again, and this time the total is 8 — the reading is again negative, and again we record it, and draw another broken line on top of the first broken line, beginning to create our hexagram from the bottom to the top.

We shake them again, drop the coins, and this time the total is 7 — a positive reading. We record this toss by an unbroken line, or a yang line repre-senting the positive principle, and the first trigram is completed.

We throw again, and once more the total is 6 and the line is negative. And again, and the total is

8 and the line is once more negative. And then we throw a final, sixth time, and the total is 9, and the line is indisputable: an unbroken, yang line goes on the top.

And so we arrive at this figure:

In order to know what it means we have to take a look at a very ancient diagram, one that may be familiar to you. Perhaps you've seen it on Chinese bowls or jewelry or carving in jade. These are the eight *trigrams* — symbols composed of three vertically stacked lines — arranged in a circle, and in the center of the design, you see the figure we saw earlier, the symbol of the yang and the yin principles.[*]

In China the symbol in the center is also known

---

[*]You will find the picture at the beginning of this section (page 66).

as *Tai Chi*, the symbol for the two fundamental principles, the positive and the negative, the yang and the yin that are held to lie at the root of all phenomena in the world. The Chinese character for the word yang looks like a fish; it represents the light side, and means the southern or bright side of a mountain. The character for yin is the black fish; it represents the shady or dark side of a mountain. Respectively, as we have seen, they represent the male and the female principles.

Notice the symbolism of a light and dark side of a mountain — you do not find a mountain with only one side; the two sides must always go together. And so, in the same way, the Chinese feel that the positive and the negative, the light and the dark, the male and the female, the auspicious and the inauspicious always go together in human life, because one cannot be distinguished without the other.

Outside the rotating figure of the positive and negative principles you will find the eight trigrams, which are every possible combination of broken or unbroken lines. These trigrams represent the eight fundamental principles or elements that, according to the *Book of Changes*, are involved in every life situation.

The one at the top, for example, means heaven, or sky, which is symbolic of the creative principle, and the one directly below means earth, and is symbolic of the receptive principle. In the Chinese system each trigram also corresponds to a family member, and the creative symbol is the father, the receptive symbol the mother.

Over on one side, we find a trigram with two yang or radiant lines enclosing a receptive line, and it is associated with the element of fire and means clinging, or perhaps holding. Opposite, the trigram has two receptive lines surrounding a receptive line, and is associated with water, and with the chasm and the dangerous abyss. Between the four cardinal trigrams appear the four intercardinal trigrams: thunder, wind, lake, and mountain. Within the oracle, every situation in life may be represented by two of these principles in preponderance. In our example above, one trigram is repeated twice, and what we have cast is a mountain over a mountain.

ADVICE FROM THE ORACLE

Altogether there are sixty-four possible combinations of these eight trigrams, which makes the meaning of each combination pretty difficult to remember. So now we will look to the *Book of Changes* itself to see what it has to say about this particular hexagram, and what advice the oracle would want to give us in answer to our question about our present situation.

The mountain over the mountain happens to be number 52, called, not surprisingly, "the Mountain." The figure of the mountain is a symbol associated with the idea of quietness, or keeping still. And when we have "keeping still" or "quietness" above "quietness," we have before us a whole emblem whose meaning is profound calm.

And so the oracle says,

THE JUDGMENT

Keeping still. Keeping his back still
So that he no longer feels his body.

He goes into his courtyard
And does not see his people.
No blame.

True quiet means keeping still when the time has come to keep still, and going forward when the time has come to go forward. In this way rest and movement are in agreement with the demands of the time, and thus there is light in life....

THE IMAGE

Mountains standing close together:
The image of keeping still.
Thus the superior man
Does not permit his thoughts
To go beyond his situation.

The heart thinks constantly. This cannot be changed. But the movements of the heart — that is, a man's thoughts — should restrict themselves to the immediate situation. All thinking that goes beyond this only makes the heart sore.[*]

You can see that this is pretty generalized advice, and it is in a way appropriate to the question because the question was vague, and so the answer is vague. But the symbolism of this answer is simply that sitting so as to keep one's back still, so that one's back is not noticed, is self-forgetfulness. And keeping one's thoughts to the immediate situation suggests the practice of meditation or calmness or quietness. That's what we're advised to do. It's good advice.

A WESTERN POINT OF VIEW

You may well say, however, that this is a thoroughly crazy way of coming to decisions, especially if I were to ask something more specific than this, or

---

[*]Reprinted by permission of the Princeton University Press from *The I Ching or Book of Changes*, the Richard Wilhelm translation, © 1950 by Bollingen Foundation, Inc.

if I had asked advice on some momentous decision I had to make. We would say, from our modern, scientific point of view, that flipping coins to come to the great decisions of life is the stupidest thing one could possibly do. After all, it neglects all rational cogitation about our situations. It takes no account of the data available in the situation. It makes no intelligent assessment of the probabilities, and before we make any important decision, we like to think over all the factors involved.

We go into the situation and think it out thoroughly. We balance the pros against the cons, and we balance assets against deficits. And therefore we believe that nothing could be more superstitious than relying upon an oracle that in turn relies entirely on the random chance of falling coins. We know that the coins have no relation to the problem whatsoever, and so naturally our contemporary point of view about this — and all other methods of fortune-telling, divination, and so on — is that if they work at all, it is nothing more than pure chance.

An Eastern Point of View

To someone who believes in this system, how-ever, perhaps a traditional Chinese or Japanese person, it does not seem farfetched at all. They might say to us, "First of all, when you consider the facts that are involved in any particular decision, and calculate all the data, how do you select which facts are most relevant?

"If you are going to enter into a business con-tract, for instance, perhaps the facts you believe pertain to this contract are the state of your own business, the state of the other person's business, and the prospects of the market, but you probably would not think about many of the personal matters that might affect the plan. And nevertheless, some-thing that you may never have considered at all may enter into the situation and change it completely. The person you're going into business with may slip on a banana peel and get seriously injured and become inefficient or even detrimental in the business. How could anyone ever predict such an eventuality by taking a sane and rational assessment of the situation?"

Or perhaps they might say to us, "How do you know when you have collected enough data? After all, the data and the potential problems involved in any particular situation are virtually infinite. What causes you to stop collecting data, or stop gathering information about how to solve a problem? I think you just collect information until you are either tired of collecting it, or until the time comes to act and you have run out of time to collect more data." And one could present a very convincing argument that because you decide when to stop investigating in a very arbitrary way, this method is just as arbitrary as flipping coins.

PROBABILITIES AND DECISIONS

"Well," we could argue, "what about probabilities? After all, we rely a great deal upon statistics in order to make decisions." But statistics have their limitations — they work very well when averaging what a large number of people are going to do, but are useless in individual cases. The actuarial tables used by insurance companies, for example, will tell you quite accurately the average life span of an adult male or female, smoker or nonsmoker, but in any individual case these tables will not tell us when someone is going to die. And the same is probably true if we look at any given decision that we may make: The probability is that we will weigh all the information, and in the final moment make our decision based upon our "hunch," which is really a gut feeling about the situation that has little to do with rational thought.

Now I am of a somewhat skeptical temperament, and I very much doubt if in fact this way of coming to decisions really works. But I say this with a certain qualification, because we can never really prove whether any method of coming to a decision really works. I may make a supremely foolish decision and as a result of it I get killed, but there would be absolutely no way of showing that my getting killed at that moment did not preserve me from a worse fate, and perhaps from making mistakes that involve the lives of many other people. If I do happen to succeed by making a right decision in business affairs and I earn millions of dollars, there is likewise no way of showing that this was not so bad for my character that it was the worst thing that could have possibly happened. So we never really know whether the outcome of a decision will be a failure or a success in the long run, because only the unknown — only what comes next — will show whether it was good or bad. And the unknown stretches infinitely before us.

DISADVANTAGES AND ADVANTAGES

There are advantages and disadvantages to both modern scientific inquiry and to the system of this old Chinese book of divination. There is a bad side to the *Book of Changes* and a distinct disadvantage in Chinese culture. The Chinese came to rely so much on the *Book of Changes* and its system of symbols for classifying all natural phenomena that in the course of time it became a very rigid structure and eventually excluded the perception of novelty.

The warning for us in this, whereby we might

take advantage of their mistake, is to realize that we are doing the same thing with scientific method. There are certain kinds of personalities who tend to become very rigid in their scientific ideas and thereafter automatically exclude certain possibilities because they do not happen to conform with alleged scientific dogma.

Take for example what we call ESP, or extrasensory perception, although I prefer to call it extraordinary sensory perception. There is extremely strong evidence that perception of this kind occurs, and yet many scientific people will ignore that evidence because they say that it simply can't happen. Limiting their inquiry in this way is to fall into the same rut that the Chinese fell into when they relied too exclusively upon the classification of the world and of events found in the *Book of Changes*.

Both systems, on the other hand, have their advantages. Just as there is a positive use for science, there is a positive side to the *Book of Changes*. The picture seen in the book through the interplay of these forms is founded on a view of life that is very suggestive to us of a new way of looking at our information, and is in accord with certain points of view that are now developing in our own science. It is a way of looking at life that focuses on not so much the causal relationship between the events, as the pattern of events as a whole.

A Comparison of East and West

Let me try to show the difference between these two ways of investigation. When we think of causality, we think chiefly of the way events are determined by the past, and by extension the way the behavior of people is determined by their past. It is as if events were a lot of different marbles that are thrown together and knock each other around. In tracing the movement of any particular marble, therefore, we will try to find out which other marbles knocked it about, and so trace its individual history further and further back. Until quite recent times the point of view of Western science was based almost exclusively on the idea of causality; it had become a study of the way things are influenced by past things.

The point of view that underlies the *Book of Changes* is that instead of trying to understand events as relationships to past causes, it understands events by relation to their present pattern. In other words, it comprehends them by taking a total view of the organism and its environment instead of what we might call a linear view. Although the Chinese have not really applied this approach to their technology, they have traditionally applied it to their art and to their philosophy of natural law, and their essential point of view is quite different from ours.

We can find a suitable analogy for the Western way of looking at things by saying that we are attempting to understand events in accordance with the order of words. I can say, "This dog has no bark," and then say, "This tree has no bark," and the meaning of "bark" in these two sentences is determined by what went before them — so if I want to know what "bark" means, I have to go back to what happened in the past.

If you look at what I would rather call the order of design, however, and not the order of words, you find a rather different situation because all of the elements of the design come at you together. They are, as we would say, "of a piece," and you see their relationship to their context and meaning all at once, much as you see the image appear when you develop a photographic plate. The meaning of each part of the design is relative to the rest of the design just as you see it at this moment.

In the same way, the fundamental philosophy of the *Book of Changes* and of the Chinese idea of the relationship between events is to understand every event in its present context. We do not understand something by what went before so much as we do by understanding it in terms of what goes with it. So the idea of the *Book of Changes* is to review through its symbols the total pattern of the moment when the question is asked, and the supposition is that the pattern of this moment governs even the tossing of the coins.

The interesting comparison that arises out of this comes about because we in the West have tended to understand events in accordance with linear or sequential orders like the order of words.

In accordance with the rules of causality, we have evolved or constructed a conception of nature based on the structure of written law.

But in the Chinese language we come again to *li*, the word for natural law that originally meant the markings in jade, the grain in wood, or the fiber in muscle, which is really the basic fundamental pattern of things. Images such as the markings in jade or the grain in wood are used because they have an extremely subtle, complex pattern that shows a large area of events all happening together at once. These patterns have to be taken in and understood at a glance, in the same way as we take in a design at a glance.

The fundamental Chinese idea of the order of nature is not compatible with formulation in the order of words, because it is organic, and is not linear pattern.

In other words, when we think of beauty we know very clearly what beauty is, but it is absolutely impossible to write down a set of laws and rules that can show us how to create beautiful objects. And mathematicians, for example, often feel that certain equations, certain expressions are peculiarly beautiful. Because they are meticulous people, they try to think out exactly why they are beautiful, and ask if we could make up a rule or formula to describe when beauty will or will not appear. Although they have proposed the criteria of elegance as a new kind of proof to be considered, their general conclusion is that if we could make up a rule and apply it in mathematics, and if we could always by the use of this rule get a beautiful result, eventually those results would cease to impress us as being beautiful. They would become sterile and dry.

And in the same way, the order of nature, the order of justice, and the order of beauty are things that we can know in ourselves, yet we cannot write down in black and white. The wiser person, therefore, is one who has the sensibility to see those things in themselves, and to know that beauty lies in the variability of experience from one situation to another.

Conclusion

Ultimately, of course, it is absolutely impossible to understand and appreciate our natural universe unless you know when to stop investigating.

In our restlessness we are always tempted to climb every hill and cross every skyline to find out what lies beyond, yet as you get older and wiser it is not just flagging energy but wisdom that teaches you to look at mountains from below, or perhaps just climb them a little way. For at the top you can no longer see the mountain. And beyond, on the other side, there is, perhaps, just another valley like this.

An old aphorism from India says, "What is

beyond, is that which is also here."

And you must not mistake this for a kind of blasé boredom, or a tiring of adventure. It is instead the startling recognition that in the place where we are now, we have already arrived.

This is it.

What we are seeking is, if we are not totally blind, already here.

For if you must follow that trail up the mountainside to its bitter end, you will discover that it leads eventually right back into the suburbs. But only an exceedingly stupid person will think that is where the trail really goes. For the actual truth is the trail goes to every single place that it crosses, and leads also to where you are standing and watching it. Watching it vanish into the hills, you are already in the truth beyond, which it leads to ultimately.

Many a time I have had intense delight listening to some hidden waterfall in the mountain canyon, a sound made all the more wonderful since I have set aside the urge to ferret the thing out, and clear up the mystery. I no longer need to find out just where the stream comes from and where it goes. Every stream, every road, if followed persistently and meticulously to its end, leads nowhere at all.

And this is why the compulsively investigative mind is always ending up in what it believes to be the hard and bitter reality of the actual facts. Playing a violin is, after all, only scraping a cat's entrails with horsehair. The stars in heaven are, after all, only radioactive rocks and gas. But this is nothing more than the delusion that truth is to be found only by picking everything to pieces like a spoiled child picking at its food.

And this is also why the Platos of the Far East so seldom tell all, and why they avoid filling in every detail. This is why they leave in their paintings great areas of emptiness and vagueness, and yet the paintings are not unfinished. These are not just unfilled backgrounds, they are integral parts of the whole composition, suggestive and pregnant voids and rifts that leave something to our imagination. And we do not make the mistake of trying to fill them in with detail in the mind's eye. We let them remain suggestive.

So it is not by pushing relentlessly and aggressively beyond those hills that we discover the unknown and persuade nature to disclose her secrets. What is beyond is also here.

Any place where we are may be considered the center of the universe. Anywhere that we stand can be considered the destination of our journey.

To understand this, however, we have to be receptive and open. In other words, we have to do what Lao-tzu advised when he said that while being a man one should also preserve a certain femininity, and thereby one will become a channel for the whole universe. And this is not just good advice for men.

Yet that is one of the misunderstandings in which I believe our culture in the West is submerged. The feminine values are despised, and we find typically among men a strange kind of reluctance to be anything but an all-male man.

But there is a tremendous necessity for us to value — alongside, as it were, the aggressive, masculine element symbolized by the sword — the receptive feminine element symbolized, perhaps, by the open flower. After all, our human senses are not knives, they are not hooks; they are the soft veil of the eye, the delicate drum of the ear, the soft skin on the tips of the fingers and on the body. It is through these delicate, receptive things that we receive our knowledge of the world.

And therefore it is only through a kind of weakness and softness that it is possible for knowledge to come to us.

To put it another way, we have to come to terms with nature by wooing her rather than fighting her, and instead of holding nature at a distance through our objectivity as if she were an enemy, realize rather that she is to be known by her embrace.

In the end, we must decide what we really want to know about.

Do we trust nature, or would we rather try to manage the whole thing?

Do we want to be some kind of omnipotent god, in control of it all, or do we want to enjoy it instead? After all, we can't enjoy what we are anxiously trying to control. One of the nicest things about our bodies is that we don't have to think about them all the time. If when you woke up in the morning you had to think about every detail of your circulation, you would never get through the day.

It was well said: "The mystery of life is not a problem to be solved, but a reality to be experienced."

The song of birds, the voices of insects are all means of conveying truth to the mind. In flowers and grasses we see messages of the Tao.

The scholar, pure and clear of mind, serene and open of heart, should find in everything what nourishes him.

But if you want to know where the flowers come from, even the god of spring doesn't know.

AN INTRODUCTION
TO MEDITATION

A L A N   W A T T S

An Introduction to Meditation
has also been published under the title
Still the Mind

*What I am really saying is that you
don't need to do anything,
because if you see yourself in the correct way,
you are all as much extraordinary phenomenon
of nature as trees, clouds, the patterns
in running water, the flickering of fire,
the arrangement of the stars,
and the form of a galaxy. You are all just like that,
and there is nothing wrong with you at all.*

— Alan Watts

CONTENTS

Publisher's Preface
Introduction by Mark Watts

Part I
The Essential Process of the World

Part II
The Essential Process of Meditation

Part III
Still the Mind

PUBLISHER'S PREFACE

By Marc Allen

Alan Watts became famous in the 1950s as a brilliant, intense intellectual, a former Episcopalian priest with a vast knowledge of both Eastern and Western religious and spiritual traditions. Unlike most of his peers, though, he embraced and actually practiced the various traditions he studied. His understanding, expressed through a great number of books and public talks, was peerless.

In the 1960s, he became a serious student of Zen Buddhism, and was a teacher — and eventually dean — at the American Academy of Asian Studies (now CIIS, the California Institute of Integral Studies). The popularity of his books and talks soared. He gave a weekly talk on San Francisco public radio that was broadcast nationally. A large number of people listened every Sunday morning; many considered it their church service.

Watts lived on a houseboat in Sausalito, just north of San Francisco, which became renowned as a center of endless discussions, parties, and meditation sessions, with famous and infamous spiritual leaders, gurus, intellectuals, writers, and others continually dropping by.

He continued to practice his meditation, and his writing and talks deepened. More and more, he was leading people into meditation and spiritual experience rather than just talking about it.

In the last years of his life, he left the houseboat and retreated to a small, isolated cabin deep in the woods. He spent nearly every morning alone, usually beginning with a Japanese tea ceremony followed by a period of meditation and contemplation. Then he would write.

His writing and speaking grew quieter and deeper. This book has been transcribed from recordings of several talks he gave in his later years. They show a maturity and an understanding of his subject that only comes after years of meditation. He had transformed over the years from a serious intellectual to a joyous, spontaneous lover of life.

His words are still leading-edge, as fresh today as when they were spoken many years ago. He is a writer and student and teacher who will be remembered, and this book shows us why:

He is able to use words to take us beyond them; he is able to instill in readers and listeners not only an understanding of meditation but an actual spiritual experience as well.

By Mark Watts

I N THE BEGINNING of *Still the Mind,* Alan Watts mentions the gift he had been given — and it was a unique gift. Watts was able to take his readers and listeners on a journey beyond the often-ignored limitations of calculation and reckoning. Perhaps the greatest part of this gift was his ability to show us how to discover simple ways of getting out of the mental trap we create for ourselves.

In our modern society, it has become apparent that the power-based world — the world of politics, government, and international finance that influences all of us — has been absolutely hypnotized and driven crazy by words and by thoughts. We have become slaves to recurring patterns in an endless stream of words. Our political leaders talk incessantly about our many problems, but it's as if they're speaking a foreign language one might call "memorandese." Almost everyone has had the experience of watching a political debate and wondering afterward what on earth the candidates were talking about. To some degree, all civilized people are out of touch with reality because we fail to distinguish between the way things are and the way they are described. For politicians this dichotomy has reached extreme proportions, but it affects everyone. We confuse money, which is an abstraction, with real wealth; we confuse the idea of who we are with the actual experience of our organic existence.

During the sixties and early seventies, Alan Watts lectured at universities and blossoming growth centers across the country. To help his audiences better understand their connection with the world, he would describe in great detail the many ways that our organic existence inseparably connects us to the entire world. Starting when I was sixteen, and on into my early twenties, I followed along whenever I could with a portable tape deck, recording his talks.

Whether the title of his talk was *Ecological Awareness, The Psychology of Mystical Experience,* or *The Practice of Zen Meditation,* he would often return to the theme of the inseparability of man and world. It was something he grasped on a deep level and could invariably help his audiences understand. His essential point was that one's actual organic being is inseparable from the universe, but the distinct idea you have of this distinct wiggle of the whole universe, which you call your body, can very easily persuade you to accept the illusion that you are a separate entity.

One reason we fall for the idea of the separate, isolated self is that, even though we admire the beauty of the natural world, nearly everyone who has grown up in Western society has certain misgivings about actually living as an integral part of nature. Instead, we adopt certain conventions that allow us to live in modern society; we cultivate our consciousness in order to "rise above" the level of natural instinct.

At one extreme, we are rugged individualists who feel the need to conquer the physical world and claim new territory for mankind. But even those who do not try to dominate the world in a physical sense may try to overcome what they perceive as their animal nature through the repression of their natural desires. We see this manifested nearly everywhere in our culture in conscious attempts to adhere to abstract ideals of virtuous living.

But as Carl Jung wrote in his essay *The Stages of Life* that "instinct cares nothing for consciousness." Like my father, Jung believed that the problems we have are manifestations of our consciousness, and more particularly, the direct result of self-consciousness and our attempt to make things better. This is at the root of so many of the dilemmas we create in so many areas of our lives.

Look at the issue of ecology, for example: Although we sincerely want to get along with nature and not destroy it, we still see ourselves as people living separately from the natural world. We are still not a part of it, due to a trick of perception that many people have called the ego. In reality the whole problem is a mental trap, and the only way out of the trap is to wake up and simply *be* in the real world.

It is necessary therefore to experience the real world directly — but here we run into a problem because some people believe that the real world is the spiritual world and others believe it is the physical world. Both of these, however, are simply ideas, concepts. As Alan Watts and so many others keep pointing out, the real art of connecting with the universe is to *stop thinking,* at least from time to time.

Practicing the art of meditation or contemplation can help us stop the perpetual chatter that goes on inside our skulls. As my father often said, "A person who thinks all the time has nothing to think about except thoughts, and lives in a world of illusions." To the degree we can stop thinking and start experiencing, we are getting back to sanity, and to reality. In meditation or contemplation we can occasionally discover a state of consciousness that is truly not self-conscious. But the only way to do this is by allowing all attempts to mentally describe the world to cease. If we talk all the time, we won't hear what anyone else has to say, and if we think all the time, we will never experience the nature of our organic existence.

In the following pages we will explore what lies at the heart of what may still to this day be considered a new way of thinking and living. As Alan Watts and many others have understood, there is nothing new in it: We are connecting — or reconnecting — with an energy as old as the universe, and with a form of wisdom at least as old as the human race, well understood by indigenous peoples and brilliantly taught by Buddhists and Hindus.

In *Still the Mind,* we are taken on an experiential journey. By participating in the experiments suggested, you will find a way to get back in touch with the reality that exists beyond our thinking — the great, unified reality our thoughts are supposed to represent but can never capture or express.

Alan Watts says it much more clearly than I do — and it has been a gratifying experience for me to spend so much time with the hundreds of hours of his words that were recorded on tape. He is a speaker and writer whose voice has continued to have a great impact many years after his passing, and I believe it is well worth spending a few quiet hours from time to time with the book you're holding in your hands. You will see how he used words and thoughts to guide us beyond our words and thoughts, and you will come to understand that we are far greater, far more miraculous in our nature than our words can express.

PART I

THE ESSENTIAL PROCESS
OF THE WORLD

CHAPTER ONE

WHO WE ARE
IN THE UNIVERSE

I WAS TAUGHT when I was a little boy that it was good to be unselfish and loving, and I used to think that I should grow up to serve other people. But after a while I found out that unless one has something to give people, there is nothing one can do to help them. Just because I thought I ought to help, it didn't mean that I had anything to give.

Gradually, over the years, as I understood what it was that I had received of significance from the world, I realized that these things were never intended as gifts to be given in the usual sense of the word. However much one enjoys the song of birds, they are not singing for the advancement of music, and the clouds are not floating across the sky to be painted by artists.

In the words of a Zen poem,

The wild geese do not intend
to cast their reflection
The water has no mind
to retain their image

When a mountain stream flows out of a spring beside the road, and a thirsty traveler comes along and drinks deeply, the traveler is welcome. But the mountain stream is not waiting with the intention of refreshing thirsty travelers; it is just bubbling forth, and the travelers are always welcome to help themselves. So in exactly that sense I offer these ideas, and you are all welcome to help yourselves.

THREE WISHES

I am offering these words for your entertainment, and to entertain myself. I am not trying to improve you, and I really do not know how I would improve you. It would be imprudent for me to recommend any improvements, because one never knows how these things may turn out — and as they say, be very careful of what you wish for, because you may get it.

One of the problems when people ask for miracles is that they never know what the miracle they ask for ultimately involves. That is why magicians and genies always grant three wishes, so that after the first two you can always use the third one to get back to where you began.

What invariably happens is that with the first wish, things never quite work out as you expected. You may not realize what it may involve if you wish for a glass to be changed into gold, for instance. If we change the arrangement of the universe in such a way that glass becomes gold, you may suddenly find that your eyesight fails or you lose all your hair, because that might go with it. We do not understand all the interconnections between things, because in reality what we call "things" are not really separate from each other. The words and the ideas about them separate them from each other, but they are not separate. They all go with each other, interconnected in one vast vibratory pattern, and if you change it at one point it will be changed at all sorts of other points, because every vibration penetrates through the entire pattern.

WHY DO YOU BELIEVE?

You never really know what is going to happen, and therefore I would not presume to say that you ought to be different than the way you are. I am not a guru, in the sense of a spiritual teacher or an authority from which you may expect something more than what you have. When you confer spiritual authority on another person, you must realize that you are allowing them to pick your pocket and sell you your own watch.

How can you be certain with any great teacher (or scripture for that matter) that they know what they say they know? You may believe in a religion; that is a choice you have made. But how do you know, and why do you believe?

If you believe in something simply because the Bible says it is true, for instance, you do so because you believe that the Bible has the authority to tell you it is true. You may well say that your fathers and mothers and all sorts of reliable people believed it, and therefore you have accepted it on their authority. If you are curious, however, you will also ask, "How did they know it was true?" Did they, by their light and example, show that they were enormously improved because of their belief?

If we look at human history with a clear eye, we see that over an appallingly long period of time people have not improved very much despite their religions and ideals. When you become a grandfather with five grandchildren as I am, you realize that you are just as stupid as your own grandfather was because you still look at things from your own limited position. And although my grandchildren may think that I am a wise and venerable man with a beard, I know that I am still a child, and I feel pretty much as I have always felt. So when you set someone up as an authority, never forget that the belief that you have in this authority is just your opinion.

IT RESTS ON OUR AUTHORITY

When De Tocqueville said that the people get the government they deserve, he was quite right. We allow the government, whether it be political or spiritual, to get away with it, and so it rests on our authority. This is true also of God. If you believe in God — that God is good, or that God is God at all — it is your opinion. And so God derives from you, and therefore this thought has some very peculiar implications with regard to the government of the universe.

Awareness of the source of spiritual authority — understanding that it comes from us, from the people — may imply that there is some sort of democracy in the kingdom of Heaven. Of course it does not overthrow God, except in the sense of a certain kind of God, and most people do not realize that there can be many quite different ideas of God.

God does not have to be a monarch; there can also be an organic god. There are also personal and impersonal gods, and there are gods that are neither personal nor impersonal. There are gods that exist and gods that do not exist, and there are gods that neither exist nor do not exist. But whatever you believe God is, it always goes back to *you*.

What Does Consciousness Rest Upon?

When his disciples approached the great Hindu sage Sri Ramana Maharshi and asked, "Guruji, who was I in my last incarnation?" he would answer, "Who wants to know?"

When they asked, "Guruji, how does one attain liberation?" he would reply, "Who is it that wants to attain?"

Who is asking the question? It always gets back to you, where it all begins — and what is that? Of course we might think we know who we are — we have been told who we are, and we bought the story we were told.

So you can't really blame anybody else for what you think of yourself. You can't go way back, in a sort of psychoanalytical way, and find the causation for what you are now. The answer is not in the behavior of your parents, or in your peer group, or whatever your situation was when you were a child, because the universe doesn't work that way. Instead it works the other way: It goes backward into the past from you, because you started it. And so when you blame somebody else for putting you into your current situation, it merely means that you have defined yourself incorrectly. Perhaps you have defined yourself as being limited to your conscious attention, and limited to your voluntary musculature. But is that all there is? Is that the real you?

What does consciousness rest upon? Have you ever asked yourself that question?

WHO ARE YOU?

Consciousness does not illumine the lamp from which it shines, just as a flashlight doesn't shine on the battery that powers it. When you make a decision, does that come from somewhere other than you? No, it comes from the depths of you, of which you are not really aware. You encompass far more than anything you know about in a conscious way.

But we are so used to thinking of "I" as simply the center of our consciousness, and the center of our will, that we ignore (or are *ignor*ant of) most of ourselves. When you think of a particular person, what do you think of? Suppose I say, "Think of your uncle," or "Think of your mother." What instantly comes to mind is their face, because we are most accustomed to seeing photographs and images of faces. When we see images of the president, most often it is the president's face, the head and shoulders, and only occasionally is the whole body seen.

What do you think of when you think of a flower? In the same way, you think mostly of the blossom, sometimes of the stalk, and occasionally of the whole plant. But very rarely when we think of a flower do we think of the flower out in a field. We would say, "That's more than the flower. The flower is not the field." But is that so? Where would the flower be without the field?

I can say in words, "The flower grows in the field."

In words I can chop the field off and say, "The flower grows," and the phrase will still make sense. However, it will not make sense in nature. If I take the field away from the flower, the flower cannot grow. The flower is connected with the field in a very deep way, and so in the same way a person is not just their head. The head has to go with the body, and the body has to go with a social and natural environment — but we never think of in that way. We know it is all there, but it doesn't come to mind automatically.

So who are you? And who decides on the limits of an organism? Who are you that gives spiritual authority to somebody else, and then pretends, "Of course it does not come from me. I bow down because I know that person really knows."?

Now the Buddhists have a very funny trick when it comes to bowing, because Buddhists do not have the idea of a supernatural authority that watches over them. So why, then, do they bow when they pay respect to a Buddha? Why do they bow when they meet you, and greet you so reverently? Bowing is paradoxically the act of a king, because it confers authority. The one who bows sets the revered image on its pedestal, and if there were no one to bow, there would be no image on the pedestal.

You put it there, but again you would ask, "How could it be so that what puts the authority up there is just poor little me, who is neurotic, or sinful, and doesn't really even understand what's going on?" But fundamentally the you that does this is the greater you, which is not just the activity of consciousness but the whole activity that expresses itself as you sit here and read this page. And what is it that expresses itself as you read? And what am I that is called Alan Watts and is offering these ideas?

I stated in the beginning that I am doing all this for entertainment, and I meant it. But who is it that is doing this for entertainment? If I say, "Alan Watts is a big act," who is it that puts on this act?

To try to trace the answer down, we might go to an astrologer and ask, "Who puts on the act?" "Well," he would say, "Where were you born, and at what time?" And he would go and look up the positions of the stars and the planets, and then he would draw a picture of my character, which just happens to be a very crude picture of the universe.

"There you are," he would say. "But I see you've drawn a picture of the universe," I would reply. That may be a surprise to him, because he probably thinks of the influences of the stars and of the planets as something that affects me, and that implies a certain separation between the bodies that cast the influences and the puppet that is influenced. But does the root of a flower influence the flower as something fundamentally different from it? No, surely the root and the flower are one process, and like your head and your feet it all goes together. In that sense then, the universe, and what you or I do, all goes together, and so that picture of the universe is really a picture of you.

We may not recognize ourselves because we think of ourselves as a chopped-off piece surrounded by our skin, and therefore we see ourselves in a rather impoverished way. And this form of perception is almost automatic. We think of ourselves as separate beings who stand alone and move through all sorts of different places but are cut off from the environment.

As a result we have an underlying feeling of alienation, of not really belonging in this universe, and we feel that we are being confronted by something that does not give a damn about us. It was here long before us, and will be here long after we are gone. We come into this world for a brief span as a little flash of consciousness between two eternal darknesses. Of course during our lives all sorts of other things go on, but nevertheless the feeling that haunts almost everybody is that this "I" is an orphan, here on a visit, and we don't feel that we really belong here.

In the same way, what do you feel when you look out at those galaxies? If you go out into a desert or up in the mountains where the sky is clear, you see this colossal affair that you are involved in. It makes a lot of people feel very small, but it shouldn't. It should make you feel as big as it is, because it is all inseparably connected with what you call *you*.

This tremendous whirling of energy is exactly one and the same energy that is looking out of your eyes, that is running along inside your brain, that is breathing, and that makes noises when you talk. The whole energy of the universe is coming at you and through you, and you are that energy.

THE NATURE OF ENERGY

"Well," we say, "but surely we die, and we disappear, we turn into dust, and this will go on long after I am gone." The whole nature of energy, however, is that it is a vibration, and a vibration is a wave, and a wave has a crest and a trough. It is like a pulse, it goes on and it goes off, and everything goes on and off.

Things like light go on and off so quickly that you can't see the off, because by definition on is always a little bit more noticeable than off. It is positive, whereas off is negative.

The outside of things is vibration, but because it goes very fast we don't quite sense it, and therefore it seems constant or solid, like the blades of an electric fan. This is true of light and also true of sound, but when you hear a very deep sound it vibrates noticeably. You can hear the texture in it; you can hear the vibrations going on and off. When you hear a great pipe organ, the whole building shudders with these vibrations. We barely notice most of the pulses, however, including the slower pulses created by the turning of the earth, the cycles of the tides, or the coming and going of the equinoxes. These are very slow vibrations, but they always go on, and then off.

We are aware of these changes only because of the contrast within them. Of course you would not know something was on if it did not occasionally go off, and you would not know it was off if it did not sometimes go on. So I have often asked the question "How would you know you are alive unless you had once been dead?"

WHERE WOULD YOU BE WITHOUT NOTHING?

Where were you before you were born?

Where will you be when you die?

We may think we will become nothing, but what we don't realize is that nothing, in its own way, is as important as something. Where would you be without nothing? What is the background to being if it is not nonbeing?

You have to have nothing to have something. It is so simple, but nobody sees it because it is fundamental to Western philosophy that out of nothing comes nothing. But how can that be? According to our logic, in order for something, or someone, to come out of nothing, there must be some kind of hidden structure inside nothing. It must contain some sort of inner workings out of which something comes. But this is not the case at all. The whole point is that there is no concealed structure, and it is just because it is honest-to-goodness plain nothing that something comes out of it. That is elementary logic, but no one sees it because everybody is afraid of nothing.

People think, "Well, if it's nothing, it will never be something again, because that's going to be the end." The theologians get this mixed up too, and even someone like Saint Thomas Aquinas believed that out of nothing comes nothing, and then he said, "God created the world out of nothing." He made a mistake because he tried to identify God exclusively with being — and of course you cannot have being without nonbeing.

The Hindus understand this, as well as the Buddhists, who inherited their philosophy and mythology. They say God is neither being nor nonbeing; it is what they have in common. Yet nobody can say what that is, and still you know perfectly well that being and nonbeing go together, like an inside and an outside, a front and a back, a top and a bottom. Being and nonbeing are polarities, like the North and South Poles. What is in between?

Nobody really knows, because you can only know what you can compare with something else. You can know something only because you can compare it with nothing, and vice versa, but nobody knows what to compare with that which is common to both something and nothing.

It is for that same sort of reason that you cannot see for yourself the color of consciousness. What's the color of eyesight? We know all of the colors because they are different from each other. We see different colors in a mirror, but what is the color of the mirror?

We may say, "Silver" — but it isn't really. Although a mirror will reflect a silver spoon as something different from something else, the mirror is a noncolor. We can't compare it with any other color, and so it is transparent to our consciousness. And like your consciousness, and like space, it is a big nothing.

Most people treat space and consciousness as if they were not there, yet suppose there wasn't any space, only solid. There would be no outside the solid, and no one would know if it was round or square because there would be nothing to compare it to, and it would be all there would be.

It would appear rather dense, but of course most of what we call something is largely nothing when you get down to atoms. Whatever it is they are really made of is vast distances apart, and when we get to the inner structure of atoms, we find precious little there. It is a lot of nothing — and this nothing turns out to be very powerful stuff.

EVERYTHING GOES AROUND

In order to have room to move around, you have to have a void to move around in, and moving around is energy, which is definitely something. So that is the sort of thing we are in, and that is the sort of thing we are. We are not just *in* it, we *are* it, and it vibrates, it oscillates, and it goes around.

The cycles are not just simply wave motions or undulations, they are also cycles of a circular kind. Everything goes around, just as when we dance we go around — and it is tremendously important to get hold of this principle of going around. We are in a phase of the life of mankind when we seem to have forgotten that cyclic quality; instead of going around we all think we are going somewhere, and that implies there is somewhere else to go. But as I wander along, I can't help but wonder where that other place would be.

HIGHER ORDERS OF BEING

In the same way, when we think of evolution, we think of a scale and of a hierarchy of different sorts of beings. We might think, for example, that above us there are angels, and then gods, and then Buddhas with attending bodhisattvas going up to we know not what heights of amazing human development. And then we think that below us are the other mammals, perhaps demons, insects, bacteria, plants, rocks, down, down to we know not what depths.

So we congratulate ourselves and say, "How great it is to be human and not to be a cat, not to be a rose, and not to be a fish." And we think how much better it will be when we can get to be angels. We human beings are very conceited, and we think we can get up there and be gods or Buddhas.

But how do you know that you are a higher order of being than a potato? What do you really know about potatoes anyway? You probably have never studied potatoes beyond knowing how to cook and eat them. That's probably about it. But have you ever thought about how a potato feels?

"Well," you say, "it doesn't feel, it's only a potato, it has nothing to feel with." But wait a minute. When you put a lie detector on a potato — some kind of skin response machine — it certainly registers, and its readings change when you do certain things. If you prick the potato, or shout at it, it will flinch. As a matter of fact, if you learn how to turn on your alpha waves and you sit beside a plant, you will find that it will pick up those alpha waves. So maybe plants are not so stupid after all.

"Well," we might say, "how can it be? It has no civilization. It has no house. It has no automobiles. It has no pianos, no art galleries, and no religion."

But the potato might say, "I don't need them. It's

you poor uncivilized human beings who have to have all this crap around you to tell you who you are and what it's all about. You are messy and inefficient, and you are cluttering up the planet with your culture. But I, the potato, have it all built into me."

"Well," we might say, "that's impossible, because you are stuck in one place all the time. How can you know anything about the world?"

But the potato doesn't need to go running around because its sensitivity extends all over the place. And so it might say, "I want to introduce you to a few things. There is my neighbor over here, the thistle. Have you ever seen how my thistle neighbor gets around? It has tiny seeds with down sticking out all over them, and when the wind comes these seeds float off into the air. And my neighbor the maple tree has little helicopters it sends off, and they spin in the air and fly away. And then I have a friend the apple tree, and it has fruit that is so delicious that the birds like it. They eat the apple and swallow the seeds, then they fly away and when they drop the seed it is sown."

These are incredible devices. Others have burrs that stick in the hides of deer, and they carry these seeds around. "This is one of the ways we get around and we spread our people so that we aren't all crowded together and don't strangle ourselves."

The potato would go on to explain, "But this is only

the beginning of the extraordinary things that we do. We have vibrations going on inside our fibers that are quite as good as anything invented by your Bach and Mozart. We enjoy this, and although you may think we are not doing anything because we just sit here all the time, we are vibrating, and we are in ecstasy. We are humming to the great hum that is going on everywhere."

Your plants may be in such an advanced state of consciousness that, unknown to you, angels are growing in a flowerpot at your door. Unbeknownst to you they may have a great deal to do with the way you think.

Consider also that the humble fly may be extremely intelligent too. With all those eyes he sees a complex relationship of perspectives, and with the ability to walk upside down on the ceiling he may have a certain perspective that is far beyond ours. Whatever do flies do when they buzz? What is it all about? We don't know, because we don't even how know to begin to study them.

It took many years to find out that bees communicate with each other by dancing, and that was such a shock that one entomologist at UCLA said, "I have the most passionate reluctance to accept this evidence."

It is a shock to find out that dolphins, for example, may be more intelligent than people, and that so-called killer whales are a very intelligent kind of dolphin. Look at those creatures. They are mammals, and it is said — although we are not sure if this is true — that they once lived on the land. Apparently they decided that being on the land is a pretty stupid way for a mammal to live, and they said, "Let's go skin diving."

They said, "You really don't have to do much for a living, and you can dance and play." And so dolphins spend most of their time simply fooling around — and they fool around in very complicated ways. If we were dolphins, we would call this art.

When we practice any art, we are in a way just fooling around. We mix a lot of paint and make beautiful patterns on flat surfaces or on textured surfaces. We put together all kinds of boxes with pluckable wires, little tubes that we can blow our breath through, and enormous tubes that we blow breath through mechanically. We stretch great taut skins that we bang with our fists or with sticks, and do all kinds of other things.

When a symphony orchestra gets up on a stage, it is essentially just a lot of baboons blowing through holes, and yet this is something very important. There is a hush, the concertmaster comes in, and everybody applauds and sits down. The concertmaster then summons the orchestra into being, and people in their tiaras and pearls and ties sit back because this is culture and this is very serious. The whole atmosphere of the concert hall is very proper, like a church.

It is a little different when a rock band takes over, and there is a light show and everything is just blowing.

This is authentic music, and it is very important music. Perhaps this is the continuation of the great Western tradition. The concert hall is good for classical music, but as the new artists take over with their rather sophisticated new music, musicians like the Beatles and the Grateful Dead continue the tradition, but it is done in a different spirit. That music is a celebration, and there is nothing sedate about it. It's music to groove with, to be right there with, because you are not pretending that you are doing something important in a solemn sense. You are doing something important because you are right in the belly of things, and you're moving with it.

All of the vegetables understand this, and so from their point of view they are very highly evolved beings. Perhaps they don't consider us inferior beings, and just regard us as something different, but we are very unfair to vegetables. When at last a human being approaches the end of life and lapses into a coma, we say, "Poor old so-and-so, he's just a vegetable." Or when somebody is lazy, we say, "They're just vegetating."

Now that shows a lack of compassion toward vegetables. The word "compassion" means to feel with, or to have passion with. If you have compassion for vegetables, or for flies, or mushrooms, or viruses, what it means is that you have put yourself in their position. When you begin to really empathize, you discover that they think of themselves as people, and they have just as much right to think that they are civilized and cultured as you and I do.

So what does that do to our perception of an ordered universe? Think about it for a moment in human terms. For one thing, most of the people we call primitive are far less violent and less diabolical than we are as a society. They live more peaceable lives, and even though the tools they use are not as developed or complex as ours, these are very dignified, civilized people. They certainly are not savage.

Many primitive peoples look at us with grave concern. They don't regard us as civilized at all. Instead they view us as a rather serious menace to the planet, because we are out of touch with the ecology of nature, and tend on the whole to be extraordinarily miserable. Some of the richest places I know of are full of wealthy people who are really amazingly miserable because, despite their tremendous resources, they are always worrying about their health, their taxes, politics, or losing their money. You can always worry about something if you are the worrying type, and it doesn't matter how rich you are or how poor you are.

A Place Called You

As you carefully observe the cycles of life, a very strange kind of relativity begins to take root in your consciousness. Everywhere on a sphere is the same place, because there is as much east of you as there is west of you, and by the same logic, any point on the surface of the sphere is the center of the circle. Furthermore, if we live in a curved space-time continuum, any planet can be regarded as the center of the whole universe, and therefore any person on a planet stands in the situation of God — as that circle whose center is everywhere and whose circumference is nowhere. So when you want to become something more than you are, different from what you are, or higher than where you think you are, all that means is that you haven't discovered where you are, and you are under the illusion that there is somewhere else that you ought to be besides here.

What we are engaging in here is a journey to the place where we are, and I would like to describe to you some of the peculiarities of this journey. It is a sort of *Alice in Wonderland* story, because it is full of paradoxes.

If I say, "We are going on a journey to where we are, a journey to the center of the universe and to the middle of space and time, and it's a place called you," people will invariably begin to pass judgment about one's progress along the way. They will say things like, "I think this person is more aware than somebody else. He's more there than so-and-so is."

Then we begin to think about the stages one goes through in getting to be more where they are than they were before. You find this particularly in sophisticated circles, where people are concerned with spiritual and psychological development, and with religion. Some very curious games are played, and many of them are forms of spiritual one-upmanship. People become concerned with being more humble than other people.

Passing Judgments

Suppose we see somebody who has a reputation, either deserved or undeserved, for being "spiritually evolved." That is the sort of phrase that is usually used. But if they get influenza and feel very sick, people shake their heads and say, "If so-and-so were really spiritual, they wouldn't be affected by sickness."

We have a funny notion in our heads that truly spiritual people are made of cast iron, that they are not sensitive, so that if you bang them about it won't affect them. But as the great Sixth Patriarch of China pointed out, you must learn to distinguish between a living Buddha and a stone Buddha, because if a buddha was simply one who was not affected by anything, then lumps of wood and pieces of stone would be Buddhas. And perhaps they are in their own way, but that wasn't the point he was making. His point was that if you think that the greatest ideal in life is to be invulnerable, then you are on your way to becoming geological rather than spiritual.

This kind of spiritual geology is very prevalent if you

know spiritual people as well as I do. I perpetually hear tales of people insisting that "my guru's better than yours." This goes on insufferably, whether it is my minister, my church, my society, or my own organization. I have heard all the reasons why, and I have heard people putting down other teachers and gurus, saying how dreadful it is that such and such a Zen master made them do so-and-so. Or we hear of the yogi who is a drunk, or sleeps with his students, or gambles, or drives cars too fast.

A great many spiritual people in this country are actually crypto-Protestants and still believe strongly in the Protestant ethic. Therefore they pass all of these judgments, despite the fact that the founder of the Christian religion said, "Judge not that you be not judged."

All the Different Performances of the Universe

If you look at all the religions and all the different kinds of practices that people are doing in the same way that you look at different kinds of vegetables and different kinds of flowers and insects and butterflies, you will see that while yogis are assuming one perspective and Baptists are assuming another, what they are all really doing is a different kind of dance — and you can accept this, and look at it with absolute amazement, and say,

"Wow, look at all these different performances this universe is doing."

If you do this, you tend to stop griping and arguing about which one is the right one. Of course, you may not accept all of the performances entirely, you may not agree with their points of view. I must admit that I have some prejudices. I don't like the flavor of some Bible Belt religions, because I find them exceedingly depressing. I also don't like boiled onions; they're distasteful as well.

On the other hand, I can worship with the Roman Catholics, and the Episcopalians, and Theosophists, and Hindus, and Muslims, and feel perfectly at ease because I find that they are all doing the same thing in different and fascinating ways. Sometimes I draw the line, but I know when I do that it is nothing more than a personal prejudice, and I am entitled to some because I am human.

After all, to be human you have to have within you a touch of rascality. When God created Adam, he put in him just a touch of the wayward spirit, in the same way that one adds a little salt to a stew. If this slight oddity, this bit of unpredictability, had not been there, nothing would ever have happened, because Adam would never have tasted the apple.

A Pinch of Rascality

Once, Carl Jung felt that he had met a man with no human failings at all, and he was terribly disturbed, because it made him feel guilty. He thought that he should probably take a closer look at himself. Then a day or two later Jung met the man's wife, and he ceased to worry about it. It wasn't because she had said, "You should know my husband is very difficult to live with." That wasn't the story at all. Instead, the wife embodied all the things that were repressed in her husband, because when you live together that intimately you begin to share your psychic life. So if one becomes too much of a light, their partner may grow compensatory and become a shadow, and vice versa. So there has to be the element of rascality — but not too much, just a pinch of it.

When I come across somebody who does not appear to have it, especially so-called spiritual people who are very pure and sincere, I always suspect they are unconscious of human nature. There is something about these solemn purists that makes me feel uncomfortable, because I like people I can let my hair down with.

THE HIERARCHY OF LIFE

You may find this is disconcerting, however, because then you begin to wonder, "Is there no perfect human being? Isn't there somebody up there, a great being who we can all look up to and respect, or are saints and saviors pretty much like anyone else?"

When you look closely at the idea of the hierarchy

of life, you realize that even someone as remarkable as Jesus Christ — who from a Buddhist point of view would be considered a great bodhisattva — can emerge at any level. According to the Buddhist idea of reincarnation, we have all occupied every position in the hierarchy, or on the Wheel of Becoming, as the Buddhists call it, since the image of time they use is a wheel. In this view, by moving around the wheel, you eventually realize that every position to which you can shift is the same position you were always in. While you are shifting you may feel there is a change going on, but once you have settled into your new position, it feels like any other settled position always felt. From the inside we know what it feels like to have a settled position because from time to time we can change — but, as the French say, the more it changes, the more it remains the same.

We who live in a fidgety culture are apt to feel that this is an awfully boring philosophy, and that we are not going to get anywhere because there is no real progress. But, on the other hand, suppose there is a possibility of real advancement and improvement. Use your imagination to the best of your ability, and figure out exactly, and in detail, where you would rather be, and who you would rather be than who you are.

If you work on this for a while, somebody who is ingenious enough will always be able to point out to you that you have left something out, and that there is something else you could improve upon. You can go on and on, and as you go about this imaginative creation of the perfect life you will eventually realize that what you are really doing is extending power.

The process is very much like the people who are now working on gene manipulation so that man can direct the future of evolution and we can breed intellectual Einsteins, physical Elizabeth Taylors, and moral Sister Teresas. All of these people had extraordinary direction as human beings by virtue of their integrity and ingenuity, and so some people may look at this idea and think it would be just great. But look how we have extended our power now. We may think it would be good to be in charge of evolution, but along comes the old problem of the three wishes again. How do we know which way is really better?

When human beings attempt to take charge of evolution, they do so using their minds and a kind of consciousness that scans the world and looks at everything serially — but the problem is that the world itself is not serial. The world is what we call multidimensional, which is to say that everything is happening all together everywhere at once, and going along much too fast for us to take adequate cognizance merely through a scanning procedure. Because scanning is confined to linear limits, it always leaves things out, and these things may be very important.

That is why, as I pointed out before, turning the glass into gold may mean that your eyesight will fail or your hair will fall out. When we bring about change with our quite limited vision, and when we change people by altering their genes, we certainly will have a new situation, but it will not necessarily be any better, because we are unable to see in advance the fullness of the role that every individual will play.

In terms of projecting power, you will see that the geneticists' power is limited because they have a limited view. If we decide to give them all the computers they need to add it all up so that they will have a complete view of life, we are then placing ourselves in a position to control life on the planet. This is to be the final creation, and we are trying to carefully arrange it with our seemingly vast intellect and omnipotent consciousness. We are to be the master magicians; we are to have complete control over ourselves, and nothing is to happen that is not in accordance with our will.

Yet suppose we do all this, and suppose we have even managed to will our will so that it is always a good will. I am not quite sure how we would know it was a good will unless there was a possibility for bad will, but suppose we have managed. Ultimately, you must ask, "Do I want to be in that kind of situation?" In other words, think of where those directions we speak of as progressive are really going, and extrapolate on them.

Perhaps you will say, "Of course I wouldn't do that, because I realize I'm never going to get there." But even so, why are you even heading in that direction? Are you sure it's a better direction to go in? After all, we kill more people with cars than we do with wars, and you have to think about things like that. I am not arguing that we should not have technological developments, but perhaps it is shortsighted to conclude automatically that they are improvements. They may not be improvements at all in the long run — and so it is very important to consider whether you want to control the direction in which you are heading.

FULL OF SURPRISES

Inwardly, do you really and truly want to have power over everything that occurs within the sphere of your consciousness? Perhaps, speaking as a man, I would like to cast a spell over a woman so that she would become exactly as beautiful as I could conceive beauty to be, and so that every inflection of her voice and gesture would obey me like a violin under the hand of a perfect master. I would entirely direct her actions, and although in her every action she would be my dream, I would quickly begin to worry about this Frankenstein woman. I would think that perhaps there was nobody home, and that all I had done was to create a machine. When I think about it, what I really want is for her to do something that I don't expect.

That is one of the reasons why it is so nice when we have an occasion to give gifts. We love surprises, because a surprise means there was someone else there, someone who made it fun by doing something that we could not have predicted.

I've heard people who think that in the future, due to our psychic development, we are all going to be able to read each other's minds. Through direct transference from one mind to another we will have access to everybody's thoughts, and there will be no privacy left. Of course, since everybody will be completely transparent to everyone else, we won't be able to surprise each other. Personally I am not looking forward to that kind of world, because I am afraid it will be quite devoid of spontaneity. We may lose that little element we call vitality.

Now this may sound as if I am saying the best sort of thing is not a universe where we realize that there is a profound underlying unity through all things, but rather a universe that is pluralistic, that is not one at all. Certainly it may be said that one of the best parts of life is having lots of separate things all surprising each other, but I see still a different scheme.

The world I see is what we might call *unity in diversity*. What we call *self* and what we call *other* are like something and nothing. They are fundamental polarities, which — just because they contrast with each other — have something in common. We cannot say what it is, though, and therefore our world will always be full of surprises.

CHAPTER TWO

MEET YOUR REAL SELF

WE HAVE STARTED out on a journey together to the place where we are. It's good to reflect, at some point along the way, on the futility of a certain kind of power game we play with our energy.

THE FUTILITY OF POWER GAMES

There are two kinds of games — the game you play to win and the game you play to play. There is a difference between the two, in the same sense as there is a difference between traveling to get somewhere and traveling just to travel, which we might call wandering.

There is a difference between motion with the objective of changing place and motion with the objective of dancing. All those forms of energy that are moving to dance, or traveling to wander, are joyous manifestations of energy. On the other hand, all those forms of energy that have us moving to get somewhere tend to become frantic, and have a quality of urgency that moves us faster and faster until we simply can't go fast enough to accomplish the object. Even when it comes to practicing meditation, people keep asking about the fastest way, and they want to know how long it is going to take.

Nishkarma means action or doing (karma) without attachment, especially without attachment to the results of action. Nishkarma is the whole point and message of the Bhagavad Gita, or "Song of the Lord," which consists of the instructions of the charioteer Krishna to the warrior Arjuna about his conduct on the field of battle. With this principle we can view not only our ordinary activities of everyday life, but also our religious activity in an entirely new way — not as something done to achieve a result.

WHY DO IT?

Of course, people then ask, "Why do it?"

People are always asking why, but one must realize that *why* is a barren question. You expect an answer addressed in terms of motivation: you want to know the cause of what somebody is doing, and the goal it leads to. If you are acting without a goal in mind, however, you can't say why you're doing it, except to do it.

Yet people are still bothered, and ask, "Why do it then?" — as if to say, "Why use energy at all? Why not just be still?" But of course that's the same as asking, "Why does the universe exist?" Why, in other words, is there motion?

The answer to that is because there is stillness. And why is there stillness? Because there is motion. In this way you reach an end to the question *why,* because it just goes around in circles.

Another way to reach an end to the question *why* is to go back into the past, because when you do you find explanations behind explanations, so that, in the words of a favorite semanticists' verse:

Big explanations have little explanations
upon their backs to bite them,
and little explanations have lesser explanations,
and so on infinitum.

In other words, you can never get there.

What happens, in fact, when we search the past to try to understand why we are doing what we are doing? What happens is that the track fades away. Look back as far as you may, but you will never find the beginning because the track gives out, just as the wake of a ship vanishes, or the contrail of a plane melts into the air.

The past, which we considered to be the push-off point, or the cause, is gone.

The real reason the past doesn't work as an explanation, however, is of course very simple: the push-off, the cause, never was in the past, it has always been in the present. It is perfectly obvious that if there was a time when the universe came into being, when it did do so, it was *now*. And that now is still here, and it is still beginning, right at this moment. So what we call the past is simply the traces, the fade-outs trailing away from the present.

So there is little point in asking why you are here, because unless you think you are here to resolve some past business — in which case you have been motivated as if you were a billiard ball hit by a cue — the issue is irrelevant.

Everybody is always talking about motivation and asking why, "Why do it?" But you can always say, "Why not?" And although that sounds a little childish by way of an answer, there *is* no why, and in a way that is rather splendid.

We tend to think that things are meaningless and dreadful if we can't explain why they happen. A policeman who pulls over a motorist who wasn't going fast enough asks, "Where are you going?" "Nowhere special," comes the answer. This irritates the policeman because he thinks you must be on the road for some reason, and that you ought to be going somewhere. If you are not, you are suspect because you're probably crazy or up to no good.

DESIRES AND DRIVES

Why do you do anything? Is it because of desire?

When people refer to their basic desires, they call them instincts, which is simply a way to label desires as drives. We all feel driven — and yet you don't realize that the energy of a drive is *you*. When you habitually abstract yourself from what you are experiencing as the experiencer or the knower of the experience, you come to feel like a puppet being driven by your emotions, or by your appetites or desires, whatever they are. But in fact they do not drive you, for there is no you to be driven by them. They *are* you.

And so this notion that leads to saying or thinking, "Excuse me, I am driven," or "Excuse me, I have to eat, I have to work, I have sexual desires" — all this is rubbish. I will not apologize for what is called "my hunger." I am very happy to be hungry, and to eat. So instead of saying, "Excuse me, but I must eat," I eat with pleasure. Look at what a degradation of ourselves that attitude carries with it, and it all comes from this feeling of being pushed or driven by something we believe is greater than we are.

The Vast Workings Underneath

The reason we feel it is greater than ourselves is because we have a conception of ourselves as nothing more than the superficial scanning mechanism called "consciousness." Of course, if that is all you are, naturally you feel driven, because you are disconnecting yourself from the vast workings that lie behind consciousness.

We disown the part of ourselves that we call instinctual, animal, or primitive. We think instead that as human beings we are the garnishing on top of the evolutionary pile. We feel we are much more evolved, not realizing that everything we have by way of consciousness and reason grows out of the primal energy that lies underneath it.

Therefore, if reason grows out of the primal energy that we are, then it means that the primal energy is at least reasonable, whatever else it may be. You can tell the tree by its fruits — for "by their fruits you shall know them" — and so it is that figs do not grow on thistles, or grapes on thorns, and a stupid universe does not create people. People are a manifestation of the potentiality in the energy of the universe, and if we are intelligent, then that which we express is also intelligent. By logical extension, that in which we express it is our central self. The world is not something external; it is what is most fundamentally you.

As long as we think we are motivated by something

external, however, and therefore feel insufficient, as long as we have that conception of ourselves, we are playing to win, because what we want is to win more, and become more. But as I pointed out, our conception or image of ourselves is only a caricature, and as such is abstract and completely inadequate. It feels as if we're insufficient in some way.

If you ask, "What did you do yesterday?" the average person will consult memory and give you a very attenuated, strung-out chronicle of events, having reduced yesterday's experience to a thin line of words. What you did yesterday becomes what you noticed yesterday, and what you noticed yesterday was a very tiny part of what happened. It was only as much as you could record in some memory code, in words or in brief impressions.

If you identify yourself with that skinny little stream of life, it is no wonder that you feel unsatisfied, because you ate the fish bones instead of the fish. And since we think that is what is happening all the time, and that life is only this skinny little thing, we feel hungry for experience, for thrills, and for ecstasy.

We say, "There must be more coming," and we need more and more future, because the past is gone, and it was a scraggly past anyway. We have no present, because life looks like an hourglass: It has a big future and a big past, but only a tiny little neck of a present that everything is squeezed through.

In Buddhist symbology the idea behind the hourglass is represented as a kind of being called a *preta*. A preta is thought of as a hungry spirit, and these creatures are represented as having enormous bellies but mouths and throats only about the diameter of a needle, so they can never get enough. That tiny mouth and immense belly represents the neck of the hourglass, and the feeling of having no present.

In fact, our present is enormously rich, and you will realize this if you understand that there is no time except present time. There is only now; there never was any time but now, and there never will be any time but now. It is all now. There is no hurry to gobble life down, and if you do you won't be able to digest it. We can go on much longer than we suppose without eating, so it's all right to just sit and be in the present.

But if you identify with the linear conception of yourself, with your story, and with the abstract ego, you feel inadequate, and therefore it becomes necessary to try to make up for that inadequacy by using energy to attain more in all sorts of ways.

WANTING MORE CONTROL

We want more control over what happens, and this leads us through a progression of steps. We start of course by attempting to acquire power in a physical way, through the possession of material wealth, historically of cattle, of slaves, of land, of crops. Then to retain all that and keep command over people's minds, we construct societies to dole out this material wealth.

But as everybody who has ever had this kind of wealth knows, it doesn't stop the feeling of inner frustration. We notice that when wealth has been in a family for a few generations, the descendants of the original robber baron become spiritual, and they go into the arts and into religion because they still feel unsatisfied. Of course, many people who have never been through the phase of having material wealth have nontheless understood that it is a blind alley, and gone into the arts or religion right away.

The First Phase of Religion: Simple Magic

Religion in its first phase, however, is what we call "simple magic" and is typified by the attempt to control the world not by the violence of arms and muscular strength, but by hypnotizing it and enchanting it. Women sometimes control men by enchanting them, and men try to control women by a similar process — and throughout history, religion has been an attempt to enchant the universe, to enchant the gods by offering sacrifices and through religious dances and rituals. Thus religion becomes magical religion.

People ask a person who goes to church, particularly

if they go to a church where they practice magic, "Why do you do that? Why do you have to do those rituals?" The answer inevitably is, in one way or another, "We perform these rites because we believe they are pleasing to God, and we have been ordered to do these things. This is the way it has been revealed that we should worship, and therefore we do it, hoping of course that God will bless us with long life, health and wealth, and sons and daughters." In this sense, all of this is still being done out of a feeling of inadequacy.

THE MORAL PHASE OF RELIGION

A more sophisticated phase of religion comes into play when the prophet finally says, "Your burnt offerings are an offense to me. Your feast days and your rites are all foolish. What I require is justice and mercy towards other people." Then religion passes from a magical phase into a moral phase, in which the emphasis is placed on living and loving, the building up of human solidarity and community.

At this level the teacher of religion becomes primarily the prophetic teacher of morals, but unfortunately you cannot love out of aridity. If you have an arid identity, you have no love to give. If you conceive yourself to be this cut-off plant that we call the conscious ego, you have no roots into a rich and luscious soil, and so all you have to give is just a little surface energy; you have no deep and abiding love.

As a result, the moral preachings are given to people who are perfectly incapable of observing them. The preachers will tell you how you ought to behave, specifically what you should do and what you should not do, but they never tell you how to become the kind of person who can do those things. And so all they succeed in is making matters worse by making you feel guilty and inadequate. You know you should do what they say, but you can't figure out for the life of you how to do it, and so you feel guilty.

A person who feels guilty feels more deprived than ever, and so has to resort to all sorts of measures to assuage their sense of guilt. Naturally this does not work, and then we begin to see that religion must involve more than moral precepts.

GRACE: THE TRANSFORMING POWER OF THE DIVINE

Religion must be a way of putting us in touch with what the Christians call "grace" — that is to say, the transforming power of the divine. Of course, they usually turn this around and say you will receive grace through magic, and so they practice the magic ceremonies of Baptism and Holy Communion. It is thought that if you participate in these ceremonies in the proper way, the magical power of God will come through and will change you. But it somehow does not seem to do so. In that situation the Buddhists and Hindus might say that the magic failed because it was not performed properly — because you were in the wrong frame of mind.

Jesus essentially said the same thing: If you will have faith, it will work. But somehow you have to find faith, and how do you find faith when you don't have it? If you ask that question of the preachers and the priests, they don't know how to answer. They may write very clever books to persuade you that God really does exist and that it is quite scientific to believe in God, but they cannot instill faith. The more cleverly you reason it out, the more all this implies doubt, and the very need to resort to clever reasoning assures us there is no genuine expression of faith.

THE PRACTICE OF MEDITATION

On this level of religion you find the quest to transform consciousness through the practice of meditation.

One may have heard that by fasting or by concentrating on breathing there is a way of opening oneself up to higher energies. One may believe that as these energies course through you they produce a magical power — and so therefore we learn what is essentially self-hypnosis, and it can do some very startling things.

However, we soon come back to the same problem we found with the geneticists, who can also do some very startling things. As all skilled technologists know, the question is, What are you going to do with it? Do you know what to do when you acquire power through meditation? How are you going to use it?

And the question still is, Who are you? Who is going to decide how to use it? Who is getting this power?

Of course, at the back of your mind you still have the attenuated and impoverished conception of you and the feeling of chronic tension that holds on tight and is the basis for the feeling of "I," of ego. There are teachers of sensory awareness who can show you how to relieve that chronic tension so you can relax and let go of the experience of being an ego for a while. That is very nice, of course, but soon afterward you relapse once again into that tension.

As long as you believe that you are your image of yourself and that you can govern your thoughts and your feelings, you will relapse into the habit of making muscular tensions to control yourself, and you will experience the ego illusion all over again. Then you may feel guilty because you are not relaxing, and the minute you feel guilty you can be certain that the ego is operating very well, although this guilty feeling means it feels injured. The ego's pride has been hurt, and no amount of guilt will get rid of the underlying problem.

At this point you may begin to realize that the meditation exercises are still a form of magic done to aggrandize yourself, and that like preachers and teachers who inculcate a sense of guilt, you are simply trying to quench thirst with salt water.

The problem is that the self-improvement approach is based on an experience of yourself that is completely inadequate. So long as you are the thinker separate from the experience of thoughts, the feeler separate from the experience of feelings, or the experiencer separate from the experience, you will feel strangled like the neck of the hungry spirit, the neck of the hourglass.

In trying to make improvements, that is the way you've defined yourself, and therefore you will not be able to use energy joyously because you will be using it with an ulterior motive. In approaching "the problem," you have defined yourself as a motivated and driven being, as a puppet.

When this illusion dissolves, however, you will discover something very strange — that meditation and religious and spiritual exercises of any kind are not necessary. People always ask if it is necessary to learn yoga breathing, or to practice tai chi, or to be psychoanalyzed. And I always ask, "Necessary for what? Where are you going? What do you want?"

Yes, if you want to get to New York it may be necessary to take the freeway. But where are you going? And what do you mean by *necessary?* Is it necessary for becoming a Buddha? Does anybody want to be a Buddha? Do you know what it means to be a Buddha?

How do you know you want to be a Buddha if you don't know what a Buddha is?

People think it would be nice to have peace of mind, to be serene, to be calm, to be undisturbed by this, that, and the other. But as long as you make all those things objects of desire, you have defined yourself as lacking them, and a person who is looking for peace is obviously in turmoil.

The person who is looking to end conflict is in conflict, and so the more you strive to stop the interior commotion, the more you are stirring it up. You are trying to smooth the waters with an iron, and it will never work.

WHY DO YOU MEDITATE?

Invariably at this point the big question arises: "If you are going to tell us that meditation is not necessary, and that it is all here and now, then why do you meditate? Why do you practice religion, perform rituals, or chant? Why do you even talk about it?"

My answer is that there is no good reason for it whatsoever. This is all a form of joyous energy, and to play with it is a form of dance. It is a great thing to do, and there are all kinds of great things to do, and we are free to explore according to our own tastes.

You can make any human activity into meditation simply by being completely with it and doing it just to do it. If you really enjoy swimming, you swim not to get to the other side of a river, or to complete a certain number of laps, or to go so far out into the ocean, or to compete in any way with yourself or with other people. You swim to experience the water rippling past you, and to enjoy the floating sensation when you lie on your back and look at the blue sky and the birds circling about. Every moment of it you are simply absorbed in this ripply, luminous world, looking at the patterns and the shifting net of sunlight underneath, and the sand way down below — that's what swimming is about.

Some of us like swimming, and in the same way some of us like religion and meditation.

A MAGNIFICENT ART FORM

We have gone through all the levels of religion until we arrive at the religion of nonreligion, where we can see that it was all here anyway and there was nothing that had to be done. In the same spirit we can then go back through the rest of life and turn it into an art form — and it is a magnificent art form.

But if you ask me why you should choose that expression rather than some other, I won't have an answer for you, except to say that getting together and meditating or chanting is what a lot of people did before they had television to absorb them.

In the jungles and on the terraces in mountain communities, for as long as anyone can remember people have gotten together to do a thing I call "digging sound." Some people still play with this sonic energy of the universe, in just the same way as I described somebody playing with the water while swimming. When these people do this, they don't worry about where they are going, or what their destiny is, or any such nonsense. Instead, they are completely alive.

A Vast Celebration

To better understand all that I am trying to say, I would like to ask if you would for the moment change your basic notions of economics — and by this I mean the economics of energy. We are always scrimping and saving because our economic models are based on scarcity rather than exuberance. But notice that the economics of nature are allegedly wasteful by our standards, and they are based on exuberance. Many more seeds than are necessary for trees and many more spermatozoa than are necessary for people are produced, and there are many more stars than anybody could conceivably want, with galaxies galore. Nature is a vast celebration of energy.

If you complain about this and say, "Oh dear me, it's all going to run out," that only means you are still looking for fulfillment in the future. Essentially you are saying, "If there is not enough future, we won't get the golden reward we are looking forward to at the end of the line."

At the heart of our economic model is a view of time that is strung out on a line, but in the natural world everything happens in cycles, which is to say in circles. Life moves through the cycles of birth, growth, flowering, and bearing fruit, which in turn casts the seed that begins life. The flowering is our symbol for the exuberance of life, and the fruits the enjoyment of its abundance.

In religious art, the golden flower represents fulfillment, and when a human being tries to symbolize what it is that they really want at the end of the line, very often they think of a flower. It is there in the celestial rose in Dante's vision of paradise, and in the golden lotus of Mahavairocana, the great Sun Buddha at the center of the mandala. There are rose windows in cathedrals, and always that flower at the end of the line.

Freud says of the flower that it is where everybody wants to go, and, being Freud, he says it is going back to the womb. What is so attractive about the womb? To explain the religious imagery of the flower by analogy with sex is only to add another puzzle. What is so great about sex? What's so great about going back to the womb? There we are regressed to the place that psychologists don't really like to talk about, and they may say that in the womb the baby feels omnipotent, but this is of course a fantasy.

We have assumed the Darwinian struggle for existence as our personality, and say of the exuberance of flowers and the abundance of fruit that they flourish only to ensure survival — but this is truly an impoverished view of life, a secular view in which the person in the world is divorced from the womb. In the womb the baby floats, and the floating baby does not know the difference between what is inside its skin and what is outside. It has what Freud calls the "oceanic feeling," and this is just another form of cosmic consciousness, only the baby does not have the language to express it like an adult. Yet there it is, drifting in the cosmic ocean — and in a way that *is* what everybody wants, because that is our original nature.

Oscar Wilde described the womb-flower of existence as "the flowers in which the gold bees dream." Yet that golden flower isn't at the end of the line — you are living in it. The radiating petals, the mandala, the great circle of the flower is the galaxy in which you live, and it is the whole universe radiating around you. Of course, this radiance is also in a cycle, and that cycling is the dance you are intimately involved in, if you can only realize that the purpose of life is not in the future.

Of course, if you think it is in the future, you will go on and on looking for it there and never find it. The future fades away in the same way the past fades out. You get older and older, and the future never comes, and you just peter out. It was never there, and you may feel vaguely cheated about the whole thing. You thought that there was something coming, that there was some great thing at the end of the line, the golden reward.

And you have been sitting in the middle of that golden reward all the time.

Now all this should be very easy to understand, unless you take a masochistic view and you feel that if you do not suffer the experience is not real. Everybody seems to be looking for new ways of suffering, as if there weren't enough in life anyway, and trying to get in touch with their "authentic" existence. But in fact, whether you're in touch with your authentic existence or not, you can't lose it, so there is no need to worry about losing the feeling of it, no need to say, "I know it's there because I've seen it once, but I am afraid I will lose the feeling of it."

Just forget about it. When you are trying to feel it — as if you couldn't — that is pushing it away. You can't get rid of your real self any more than you can get rid of now. It *is* you. It's your being — to be more accurate, your being is not your being, *you* are the being. It doesn't matter if you live or die; it doesn't make the slightest difference. It is nothing just as much as it is something, and nothing and something are simply the alternations and the vibration of energy.

What Does It Feel Like at This Moment?

How are you feeling now? Just feel yourself. What does it feel like just to be here now? Just feel the feeling — and can you feel, in addition to this feeling, someone feeling it, or is that the same as the feeling?

Some of you may have what you would call negative feelings — depression, anxiety — and you may feel tension in the chest, a funny feeling in the stomach, or pressure in the head. Or if you are sick in a chronic way, you may feel trouble from the center where the sickness is located. But, at this moment, don't name that feeling — just explore it. It is there, whatever it is. Now you may want to change that feeling, but suppose you can't. For a while you may be able to think about something else, but now let's say to ourselves, "I feel the way I feel, and I can't really do much about it." As we have seen, that is because the "I" that is supposed to be separate from and controlling the feeling is only imaginary.

Inner and Outer Worlds

So if that is the case, then what you are is the totality of this present experience — the inner feelings, the discomfort and rumblings and pulsations inside your organism, together with your outer feelings, because actually your outer sensations are happening inside your brain. What you see out in front of you is the state of your optical nerves, which are inside your head. What you hear is the state of your auditory nerves, which are inside your head. So inner and outer are really so mixed up with each other that there is no difference.

The skin is the bridge between the world "inside the skin" and the world "outside the skin." But there would be no external world if there weren't an internal one, and vice versa. Your internal world is in my external world, and my internal world is in your external world. It all goes together in a great mixed sensory field where everything is essential to everything else, like backs to fronts and fronts to backs.

So here it is, and you can feel everything happening. Your breath is going along. Your ears are working. The people across from you are moving, the trees and buildings are coloring and shaping. It is all that kind of a happening.

Now we can equally well define this happening as your doing. This whole happening that is going on — that is you, if there is a you, a self, in any sense whatsoever. So if you try to change it, you are differentiating yourself from it. You are standing away from it and, in that moment, you split the unity.

But don't worry if you find yourself habitually

standing away from it. Simply treat that as part of the happening. If you can't stop standing away from it — objectifying it, as it were — that is also part of the happening and it is going on. If there are some things you can't accept, and you are fighting them, that fighting is part of the happening too. So don't try to interfere with it, just let be whatever is.

There is no hurry, and no place else to be. I suppose you can go away if you want to, if you are nervous and want to do something else. But has it occurred to you that there may be really nowhere to go, because you take yourself with you if you go somewhere else? And if you have a problem here, you will have a problem somewhere else, because you are the problem. So there is no hurry, and in a way there is no future. It is all here — so take it easy, take your time, and get acquainted with it.

Watch Quietly

Just watch quietly this "going on." Whether you close your eyes or keep them open makes little difference. You find yourself once again tending to put names, words, descriptions on everything that you experience, and that's not necessary. Don't try to stop yourself putting names on things, just regard your doing that as an activity that is happening, like the sound of a car going by. If you ask, "Why am I doing this?" just hear the sound — "why am I doing this, why am I doing this" — as "da da da, dadada."

When you feel those outside sounds and activities and motions, they may seem strange because they are no longer under your voluntary control — but neither are your belly rumbles or the mechanisms of your optical nervous system. None of this is under your control, but it is all definitely you. The idea that you control something really isn't under your control either, because when we move our fingers, we're using energy, but we don't control that energy. Our thoughts are just energy too — it is all bubbling up in us, and we don't know why.

In the same way, all the happenings that are by social definition outside your skin — not under your voluntary control and so not you — are just as much you as the belly rumbles and the energy bubbling up inside you. This whole experience is you going along, and if you try to control it, you will again begin all sorts of absurd straining, like trying to lift an airplane off the ground by pulling at your seat belt. So just let all this that you are feeling happen, because in fact there is nothing else you can do. There is no choice; it is going to happen anyway.

Your Full Body, Your Real Self

Now in this state it is your full body that you are experiencing, the whole body of your experience.

In the Far East, the Buddhists say that our full body, our real body, is composed of a trinity of three bodies: *Nirmanakaya* is the functioning body, the physical body with which we usually identify. *Sambhogakaya* is the body of our mental and emotional activity, and it is our capacity to enjoy, for it is the energy of eternal delight. *Dharmakaya* is our ultimate body, our real body, which consists of nothing less than the whole quantum field of the universe, for, in truth, we are One with All That Is.

Feel it, it is happening.

Your wandering thoughts are just happening. The buzz in the head is just happening. There you are.

It is not being pushed around by anything. It is the big happening, and that means it's free. It isn't happening *to* you, it is you happening, and that's the difference.

Meet your real self.

PART II

THE ESSENTIAL PROCESS
OF MEDITATION

CHAPTER THREE

THE PHILOSOPHY OF
MEDITATION

I AM BY NATURE a person who has the fundamental feeling that existence is extremely odd.

Other people apparently think that existence is quite even — that is to say, ordinary — and not to be questioned, but I have always had in the bottom of my heart the sense that it is very strange indeed that I am here at all. The feeling of "I" gives me what I can only describe as a funny feeling, and I do not take it for granted.

This feeling is not something that I can just toss off, and then go on with my everyday business — and yet the curious paradox of this is that, at the same time, I do not take it seriously. On one hand I have the feeling that to be alive, to participate in this universe, is so wonderful I simply don't know what

81

to say about it, but on the other I can't identify myself with any of the parts or the social roles that people play.

THE PROBLEM WITH EXISTENCE

There does seem to be a problem with existence, and with being alive. What that problem is about, at the sort of nitty-gritty level, is the very basic idea in our thinking that one must live, that we need to survive to go on, and therefore we need money for food and shelter. We feel we must go on, even though we know that we are not going to get away with it for very long, and we know that after a certain number of years we are going to die and that this thing we call life is going to end.

When life ends the thing that we call "I" is going to go somewhere else, maybe into a deep sleep, maybe even without dreams. Between now and that inevitable event we may experience the most ghastly pains — not only the pains of physical disease, or of being wounded or hurt, but perhaps the pains of worrying about the failure of our responsibility to people who depend on us. So we suffer other people's suffering simply because we are sensitive and have imagination; we do it so much that our adrenaline levels respond simply by imagination to the sufferings of other people.

Obviously all these problems cannot be solved on the physical level — we don't expect in our lifetime that medical skill will make us exempt from death. We also don't seriously expect that human beings will all learn to be nice to each other, and will refrain from war, racial prejudice, and horrors of that kind. We don't seriously expect to find a method of being protected against all possible disease and pain by taking some sort of drug.

ANOTHER WAY AROUND THESE PROBLEMS

Over the years I have begun to wonder if there is another way around these problems. Perhaps instead of resolving these issues at the technical level, we could solve them at the psychological and spiritual levels by disciplining ourselves so that we wouldn't be afraid of them anymore. And so, in accord with that motivation, we seek out spiritual and psychological teachers.

We wonder if we could somehow be made over so that we would not have to worry about our problems. But if you examine the desire to overcome this mess through a spiritual discipline, you will see that this wanting to overcome the mess and not to have it anymore is precisely the mess. The thing that we object to about ourselves is precisely what we continue to do in our attempts to overcome it; in other words, the activity that we employ in overcoming the mess is the mess that we object to. It is very important to realize this, and if you do realize it, it raises the question "Then what can I do?" What can I do to transform this quaking mess into the state of mind of the true mystic?

Now, if you are the mess, there is obviously nothing that you can do to transform yourself into the state of mind you idealize as that of a true mystic, a saint, or even the Christ. But by pursuing this line of thought you may realize that all your ideals are simply manifestations of the mess trying to get away from itself.

You are put in the position of feeling that it is absolutely necessary to be different from the way you are, but there is absolutely nothing you can do about it because being the way you are, you can't be different from your self. It's as if one were to say, "I know that I shouldn't be selfish, and I would very much like to be an unselfish person, but the reason why I want to be an unselfish person is that I am very selfish. And really I would love myself far more and respect myself far more if I were unselfish."

The same is true of people who believe that they ought to love God. One might well ask, "Why do you want to love God?" And the answer is invariably, because God is the most powerful ruler, and it is always best to be on the side of the big battalions. Most often that is the real reason why people believe in God, and it comes down to the fact that they are looking out for the safety of their own spiritual skins.

All sophisticated saints have known this, including Saint Paul, Saint Augustine, and Martin Luther. None of these great men knew what to do about this contradiction, because if people believe in it there is really nothing to be done. But apparently something has to be done — however, when you really look into yourself, you realize there is nothing you can do. There is nothing anyone can do to be anyone else than who they are, or to feel any other way than the way they feel at this moment.

We are this mess that has the capacity to know the horrors of what life can do to us — yet this is not as much of a blind alley as it seems to be. If you discover yourself in a blind alley, or even a cul-de-sac, the fact that you found yourself there will invariably tell you something.

Watch the flow of water when it floods an area of land and you will see that it puts out fingers, and some of them stop because they come to blind alleys. But the water doesn't pursue that course; it simply finds its way around. The water never uses any effort, however, only its weight and gravity, and by following its level it finds the path of least resistance.

As human beings we do the same thing, and when we think that we have come to a dead end or a blind alley we try to find another way around. Suppose the water, when it reaches a place where a finger of water stretches out over dry ground and doesn't go further, were to say to itself, "I failed!" Why, we would say it was just being neurotic. "Just wait," we would advise, "and you will find the way to get through."

Now when you discover that you are like the water, and that there is no way of transforming yourself, you become a fearless, joyous, divine being, as distinct from a quaking mess.

When you see that there is no way, it is not a gloomy realization, but a very important communication. It is telling you something in the same way that the land is telling the water this is not the way to go. It is really saying, "There is another way — try over here."

Sometimes life is telling you that the course you are on is not the way to go, and the message underlying all of this is that you cannot transform yourself. Life is giving you the message that the "you" that you imagine to be capable of transforming yourself does not exist. In other words, as an ego, I am separate from my emotions, my thoughts, my feelings, my experiences. So the one who is supposed to be in control of them cannot control them because it isn't there. And as soon as you understand that, things will be vastly improved.

What Do You Mean by the Word "I"?

Now we can go into this and ask, "What do you mean by the word 'I'?" We are going to try some experiments on a number of different levels, first in the ordinary way: What do you mean by the word "I"? I, myself. Your personality, your ego — what is it?

First of all, it is your image of yourself, and it is composed of what people have told you about yourself. Who you are is based upon how others have reacted to you, and what sort of impression they have given you of the kind of person you are. Your education plays into the process as well, and out of all this an ego emerges that is a conceptual expression of who you think you are. The style of life you then live is a reflection of this image.

But remember, it is an image — just an idea. It is your thoughts about yourself, but in fact you are not this at all. Your total physical organism, your psychological organism, and forces beyond that are all you, because an organism doesn't exist as an isolated entity any more than a flower exists without a stalk, without roots, without earth, without the environment.

In the same way, although we are not stalked to the ground, we are nevertheless inseparable from the world around us, and from a huge social context of parents, siblings, and people who know us and work with us. It is simply impossible to cut ourselves off from either our social environment or our natural environment. We are all that, and there is no clear way of drawing the boundary between this organism and everything that surrounds it.

And yet, the image of ourselves that we have does not include all those relationships. Our idea of our personality and of ourselves includes no information whatsoever about the hypothalamus or even the brain stem, the pineal gland, the way we breathe, how our blood circulates, how we manage to form a sentence, how we manage to be conscious, or even how we open and close our hands. The information contained in your image of yourself says nothing about any of this.

Therefore it is obviously an extremely inadequate image, but nonetheless we do think that the image of self refers to something because we have the very strong impression that "I" exist. And we think that this impression isn't just an idea, it is really substantially there, right in the middle of us. And what is it?

What do you actually sense? When you are sitting on the floor, you feel the floor is there and is real and hard. What is the "you" sitting on the floor, and what do you have the sensation of when you know that it's you, right here? What is it?

First of all, let's ask, "In what part of your body do you feel your self — the real "I" — exists?" We can explore this question very deeply, and maybe you want to think about it for a moment before I suggest a preliminary and superficial answer:

The sensation that corresponds to the feeling of "I" is a chronic muscular tension in the body, which has absolutely no function whatsoever.

What do you do when you try, or concentrate, or

pay attention? When I was a little boy in school I sat next to another boy who had great difficulty in reading. And as he worked over the textbook with its perfectly piffling information, he groaned and grunted as he read, trying to get the sounds out, as if he were heaving enormous weights with his muscles. The teacher was vaguely impressed that he was trying, and although he seemed to be making a tremendous effort, all of his straining had absolutely nothing to do with getting anything done.

Tying yourself up into a knot has absolutely nothing to do with the way your mind works. If you try very hard, and look very intensely, perhaps you will tighten the muscles around your temples, and maybe clench your jaw a bit, but if it does anything, it will just make your vision blurry. If you want to see something clearly, you relax, and instead of making an effort you simply trust your eyes and your nervous system to do their job.

The other night I was writing and I completely forgot somebody's name, but I knew that eventually my memory would produce it. I just sat for a while and said to my memory, "You know very well who this person is, please give me the answer." And there it was, because that's the way nerves work. They don't work by forcing themselves, and yet we've all been brought up to try to force our nervous activity, our concentration, our memory, our comprehension, and indeed our very love.

We have tried to force it with our muscles — and men will understand me if I say you can't force yourself to have an erection by muscular effort. Women will understand me if I say you can't force yourself with muscles to have an orgasm — it just has to happen, and you must trust it to happen. There is absolutely nothing you can do about it by using your muscles. In much the same way, the notion that we have of ourselves, of ego, is a composite of an image of ourselves that doesn't fit the facts, and a sensation of muscular straining that is futile. When you come down to it and take a closer look, what you conceive to be yourself is the marriage of an illusion and futility.

WE ARE NO LESS THAN THE UNIVERSE

Well what are we, if we aren't who we think we are? When you take a scientific point of view, your organism is inseparable from its environment, and so you really are the organism/environment. In other words, you are no less than the universe, and each one of you is the universe expressed in the particular place that you feel is here and now. You are an aperture through which the universe is looking at itself and exploring itself.

When you feel that you are a lonely, put-upon, isolated little stranger confronting all this, you are under the influence of an illusory feeling, because the truth is quite the reverse. You are the whole works, all that there is, and always was, and always has been, and always will be. But just as my whole body has a little nerve end centered here, which is exploring and which contributes to the sense of touch, you are just such a little nerve end for everything that is going on. Just as the eyes serve the whole body, you serve the entire universe. You are a function of all that is.

Yet if this is so, the facts just do not fit the way we feel, because we feel it the other way around: "I am a lonely little thing out here exploring this universe and trying to make something out of it. I want to get something out of it and do something with it. And I know I am going to fail because I know I'm going to die one day." So we are all fundamentally depressed, and as a result think up fantasies about what is going to happen to us when we are dead, and try to make ourselves feel better about it.

But if you are essentially the universe, what is going to happen to you when you are dead?

What do you mean by *you?* If you are the universe, in the greater context that question is irrelevant. You never were born and you never will die, because what there is, is you. That should be absolutely obvious, but from an egoistic perspective it is not obvious at all. It should be the simplest thing in the world to understand that you, the "I", is what has always been going on and always will go on, coming and going forever and ever.

We have been bamboozled, however, by religionists, by politicians, by our fathers and mothers, by all sorts of people who tell us, "You're not it." And we believed it.

So, to put it in a negative way, you can't do anything to change yourselves, to become better, to become happier, to become more serene, to become more mystical. But if I say you can't do a damn thing, you can understand this negative statement in a positive way. What I am really saying is that you don't need to do anything, because if you see yourself in the correct way, you are all as much extraordinary phenomena of nature as trees, clouds, the patterns in running water, the flickering of fire, the arrangement of the stars, and the form of a galaxy. You are all just like that, and there is nothing wrong with you at all.

An Element of Doubt

You may have an element of doubt in you, however. We all object to ourselves in various ways, and in a sense there is nothing wrong with that either, because that is part of the flow, of what is going on. That is part of nature, and a part of what we do. To deliver you from the sense of guilt, I am going to teach you that you needn't feel guilty because you feel guilty.

They taught you as a child to feel guilty, and you feel guilty — that's no surprise. If somebody comes along and says you shouldn't, that is not the point. I am not going to say that you shouldn't — but I say that if you do, don't worry about it. And if you want to say, "But I can't help worrying about it," I'm going to say, "Okay, go ahead and worry about it."

This is the principle called judo in Japanese, which means the gentle way. Go along with it, go along with it — and then you can redirect the energy to go your own way.

The most interesting thing you can do in life is really the most natural thing to do: to call into question the rules of the game. If we say, "Let's all be honest with each other," what do you mean by honesty? Do you know what the truth is?

If you call these things into question, a curious thing happens, and that is that nobody knows what they are supposed to do. And this is the most embarrassing situation in life. When we are all here and we don't know what we're supposed to do, now we are really up against our view of reality.

THE ESSENTIAL PROCESS OF MEDITATION

This is the beginning of meditation. You don't know what you're supposed to do, so what can you do? Well, if you don't know what you're supposed to do, you watch. You simply watch what is going on.

When somebody plays music, you listen. You just follow those sounds, and eventually you understand the music. The point can't be explained in words because music is not words, but after listening for a while, you understand the point of it, and that point is the music itself.

In exactly the same way, you can listen to all experiences, because all experiences of any kind are vibrations coming at you. As a matter of fact, you are these vibrations, and if you really feel what is happening, the awareness you have of you and of everything else is all the same. It's a sound, a vibration, all kinds of vibrations on different bands of the spectrum. Sight vibrations, emotion vibrations, touch vibrations, sound vibrations — all these things come together and are woven, all the senses are woven, and you are a pattern in the weaving, and that pattern is the picture of what you now feel. This is always going on, whether you pay attention to it or not.

Now instead of asking what you should do about it, you experience it, because who knows what to do about it? To know what to do about this you would have to know everything, and if you don't, then the only way to begin is to watch.

Watch what's going on. Watch not only what's going on outside, but what's going on inside. Treat your own thoughts, your own reactions, your own emotions about what's going on outside as if those inside reactions were also outside things. But you are just watching. Just follow along, and simply observe how they go.

Now, you may say that this is difficult, and that you are bored by watching what is going on. But if you sit quite still, you are simply observing what is happening: all the sounds outside, all the different shapes and lights in front of your eyes, all the feelings on your skin, inside your skin, belly rumbles, thoughts going on inside your head — chatter, chatter, chatter. "I ought to be writing a letter to so-and-so.... I should have done this" — all this bilge is going on, but you just watch it.

You say to yourself, "But this is boring." Now watch that too. What kind of a funny feeling is it that makes you say it's boring? Where is it? Where do you feel it? "I should be doing something else instead." What's that feeling? What part of your body is it in? Is it in your head, is it in your belly, is it in the soles of your feet? Where is it? The feeling of boredom can be very interesting if you look into it.

Simply watch everything going on without attempting to change it in any way, without judging it, without calling it good or bad. Just watch it. That is the essential process of meditation.

CHAPTER FOUR

THE PRACTICE OF
MEDITATION

WHAT WE CALL MEDITATION or contemplation — for want of a better word — is really supposed to be fun. I have some difficulty in conveying this idea because most people take anything to do with religion seriously — and you must understand that I am not a serious person. I may be sincere, but never serious, because I don't think the universe is serious.

And the trouble comes into the world largely because various beings take themselves seriously, instead of playfully. After all, you must become serious if you think that something is desperately important, but you will only think that something is desperately important if you are afraid of losing it. In one way, however, if you fear losing something, it isn't really worth having. There are people who live in dread, and then drag on living because they are afraid to die. They will probably teach their children to do the same, and their children will in turn teach their own children to live that way. And so it goes on and on.

But let me ask you, if you were God, would you be serious? Would you want people to treat you as if you were serious? Would you want to be prayed to? Think of all the awful things that people say in their prayers. Would you want to listen to that all the time? Would you encourage it? No, not if you were God.

In the same way, meditation is different from the sort of things that people are supposed to take seriously. It doesn't have any purpose, and when you talk about practicing meditation, it's not like practicing tennis or playing the piano, which one does in order to attain a certain perfection. You practice music to become better at it, maybe even with the idea that you may someday go on stage and perform. But you don't practice meditation that way, because if you do, you are not meditating.

THE PRACTICE OF MEDITATION

The only way you can talk about practice in the context of meditation is to use the word *practice* in the same way as when somebody says that they practice medicine. That is their way of life, their vocation, and they do it nearly every day. Perhaps they do it the same way, day after day — and that's fine for meditation too, because in meditation there is no right way and there is no idea of time.

In practicing and learning things, time is usually of the essence. We try to do it as fast as possible, and even find a faster way of learning how to do things. In meditation a faster way of learning is of no importance whatsoever, because one's focus is always on the present. And although growth may occur in the process, it is growth in the same way that a plant grows.

THE PERFECT PROCESS OF GROWTH

Once upon a time in China, there was a farming family, and they were having dinner. The oldest son came in late, and they asked him, "Why are you late for dinner?"

"Oh," he said, "I've been helping the wheat to grow."

They came out the next morning and all the wheat was dead. It turned out that the son had pulled each stalk up a little bit, to help it grow.

The point is that growth always occurs in a being as it does in a plant, and it is perfect at every step. No progress is involved in the transformation of an acorn into an oak, because the acorn is a perfect acorn, and the sapling is a perfect sapling, and the big oak tree is a perfect oak, which again produces perfect acorns. At every stage perfection is there, and it cannot be otherwise.

Practicing meditation is exactly the same. We should not talk about beginners as distinct from experts, and we should develop, if we can, a new vocabulary because it is very difficult in the context of our competitive world to speak about things like this. To bring across the idea of doing something that is not acquisitive — something you are not going to get anything out of — is difficult. And it's even more difficult when there is no one to get anything. When "you" understand the art of contemplation, there is no experiencer separate from experience, and there is no one to get anything out of life, or therefore to get anything from meditation.

REVERSED EFFORT

We have a principle here of reversed effort, something to understand as a background to anything said about techniques — because whenever we talk about techniques, we seem to be talking about the competitive, and about mastery. The idea of mastery of technique is very important if you play a musical instrument, because technique is the key in the making of a satisfactory sound. But if you force the learning of technique, or force the performance of it, everyone will hear it, and you will hear the forcing yourself.

To be musical you have to address yourself to the

playing of an instrument without hurrying, and without forcing anything. You will find there is a point then where the instrument seems to play itself, and when you get the peculiar feeling that the sound coming out of a flute or a violin string is happening of itself. Then you are playing the instrument properly.

It's the same when you sing: there comes a point when your voice takes over. This is the difference between perspiration and inspiration.

You may say, as Christians do, that the act of worship is inspired by the Holy Spirit. When monks are chanting, they believe that the Holy Spirit is chanting through them, and they are flutes for the Holy Spirit. This is a very precise and particular phenomenon because there is a way of resonating the breath and of harmonizing sound so that it comes of itself and you don't do it. We attribute that way of producing sound to the "Holy Spirit," but it is based on breath.

WATCHING BREATH

Breath is a curious operation, because it can be experienced as both a voluntary doing and an involuntary happening. You can do a breathing exercise and feel that "I am breathing" in just the same way as you can feel "I am walking." Yet on the other hand, you breathe all the time when you are not thinking about it, and in that way it is involuntary. You must breathe —

and so it is the faculty through which we can realize the unity of the voluntary and involuntary systems.

In Buddhism, this is called mindfulness of the breath, or watching breath. And watching breath is fundamental in meditation because, like sound, it is easy to see the happening in it, as distinct from what we thought of as the doing of it. Breath happens, but the curious thing is that you can get with the breath, and in getting with it, extraordinary things can happen.

Anyone who swims knows this, and anyone who sings knows that breathing is important. In archery, in any athletic discipline, the alignment of body and breath is critical. The synchronization of what you are doing with your breathing is the whole art. But powerful breath is not accomplished through muscle power. It is accomplished by gravity, by weight.

A MEDITATION EXERCISE

I would like you to sit upright, either in a comfortable chair or on the floor on a cushion or pillow. The reason for sitting straight is so the part of your body in which the breathing is occurring is unencumbered. Also, when you sit upright on the floor you are slightly uncomfortable, and you won't go to sleep, because in any peaceful and quiet state of mind it is very easy to go to sleep.

Now in this position, simply become aware of your

breathing, without trying to do anything about it at all. Let it happen, and watch it.

At the same time, let your ears hear whatever they want to hear. In other words, let them hear in the same way you are letting your lungs breathe.

Now beyond this, you can breathe out by letting the breath fall outward without pushing it, and as you get to the end of the out breath, let go with the same sort of feeling that you have when you let your body drop into a very comfortable bed — let it drop out and fall. Let the weight of the air do it. Don't push, drop. Then after a while, the breath will return. But don't pull it in, let it fall back in. The breath will drop in until you've had enough; then let it drop out again.

It's a good idea in this exercise to breathe in through the nostrils and out through the lips, allowing there to be a slight sensation of moving air on your lips so that you know you are breathing. Never force anything — just have the feeling of going this way and that way by virtue of weight, and of gravity.

Adding Sound

Then, if you wish, as you let the breath fall outward, you can simply float a sound on it. First, you can just do this mentally. Think of a sound that pleases you, a note that seems agreeable to your voice. As you breathe out heavily, imagine that sound to yourself, whatever sound you feel like. Now if you've got a humming sound in mind, on the next round of the out breath, hum it out loud, and keep it going.

At first you may be a little short-winded and uneasy about something like this. As well as allowing the sound to hum and happen with the breath that is falling out, you can, as it were, simply request it to increase in volume without forcing it.

And when your sound ends, bring it in again quite softly, and then allow the volume to rise. You will get an almost continuous sound, and if you do this in a group, the sounds will run together.

Try it now, if you wish, picking your own note.

Try it again, once more.

Now ask it to increase its volume. Listen a moment. What we are working into is the completely liberated, yet soft and gentle, act of letting sound happen through us without the slightest sense of strain, so that you are not singing it, but it is singing with your voice.

Don't premeditate a tune, but let it come, so that it's almost as if you were talking nonsense. Let it play gently with your voice. You are simply preoccupied with it, like easy humming to yourself.

Hmmmm....
Or, *Ahhh....*
Or, *Oooommmm....*

When you are thus absorbed in sound, where are you?

You are in a state of consciousness that is, even at first, at least a primitive form of *samadhi;* that is to say, we are happily absorbed in what we are doing, and we have forgotten about ourselves. You can't very well do that and still worry or think about anything serious.

Notice that there is a special way of doing it. We can get wild with it and do a kind of Native American chant or one of the more vigorous and forceful Tibetan Buddhist chants, but that form of chanting can be straining, unless you're in a large group and can soar on the group's energy. If you keep it down to a soft tone, you will find the floating feeling of the voice. If you feel any sound that is uncomfortable, you can instantly avoid it. Slip down if you are going too high, or slip up if you are getting too low. If your voice tends to change, follow its change, so that you are just going along with it.

THE DIVINE ELEMENT

This is why, from ancient times, people have discovered humming and singing, and everybody used to sing while they worked. But you'll notice that today very few people sing at all; you have to make a point of it. People are afraid of their voices — that is, their melodic voices as distinct from the spoken voice. I know an enormous number of people who never sing at all.

In India to this day when the scriptures — the Upanishads and the Sutras — are read, they are invariably chanted, because as soon as you bring a note into it an extra dimension is added to the voice. That is the divine element, which is symbolically the singing sound of the universe.

This is a form of what I would call free mantra chanting, which isn't used much. But as you do it, it will give you a very good idea of what the meditative state is. It isn't just letting things going on around you happen, it is inside you as well. In free mantra, as distinct from prescribed mantra, each spontaneous chant has a different feeling to it.

The Tibetan monks go down to an extraordinarily deep sound — they go as deep as one can get. There is a reason for this, but it is very difficult to explain because you have to do it to understand it. But when you get as deep down into sound as you can go, you are going to an extreme of the vibration, and you feel naturally that what is deep is part of the underpinnings, the foundation. When monks go into that deep sound, they are literally exploring the depths of sound, going into it deeply. They will get down somewhere on an *Om,* and take it to what feels like the center of the earth.

When you try the meditation we have just been through with sound, you might sometimes find that you hear your voice go wrong, but you always get a sensuous feeling of the breath, and of course it is very enjoyable to breathe. You will find this enjoyment will help in the quality of the sound you produce — although we have to get away from some of our musical prejudices when we do this. You can make up your own nonsensical mantras, and there are lots of traditional mantras as well. But to make one up, just absorb yourself in a vibration that gets you going and then play with it.

Play with the sound you are making, and when you stop you will still feel the pulse going through you. These sounds are easy to run along with.

Deep Listening

Some people think that to spend a lot of time gently humming nonsense to yourself is a waste of time. But ask yourself, What are you going to do with the time that you save?

With all this, the first thing we have to understand is what I call deep listening. Very few people ever really listen, because instead of receiving the sound, they make comments on it all the time. They are thinking about it, and so the sound is never fully heard. You just have to let it take over, let it take you over completely, and then you get into the *samadhi* state of becoming it.

This also means that you abandon your socially nervous personality. One of the reasons why people don't sing is that they hear so many masters performing on records that they are ashamed of their own voices. You may think there's no point in singing unless you are good at it, but that is like saying there is no point in doing anything at all unless you are particularly gifted at it, which is ridiculous. Of course singing is very good for you, but we won't dwell on that because it brings too much purposiveness into it — having to fulfill a conscious purpose and design.

ANY SOUND FROM THE SOURCE

Instead we are like children making noises because of the absorbing sound they produce. Children make all sorts of noises to explore the possibilities of what they can do with their voice. But you don't see adults going around humming and burbling, even though it is tremendous fun. All of this is perfectly at home within meditation.

Joshu Sasaki, a Zen master from Los Angeles, tells his students to stand up and laugh for five minutes every morning because that's a better form of meditation than sitting for a long time getting sore legs. It embarrasses the hell out of some people to even try it, and instead when they see someone doing it they ask, "What are you laughing at? You know I don't see any point in laughing unless there's something funny."

I had a friend, a very fat friend, and he was a theological student. He used to take the elevated train that went from Evanston into Chicago and sit in the middle of the car where everybody could see him. He would sit there with a kind of vacant look and chuckle to himself. And slowly he'd work it out, laughing louder and louder with all his flesh vibrating. By the time they got to Chicago, the whole car was inevitably hysterical with laughter.

I tell you this story to illustrate that any sound you feel coming from the inside can be used as mantra meditation, and the deeper the source, now matter how ridiculous, the better.

PART III

STILL THE MIND

CONTEMPLATIVE
RITUAL

FOR A LONG TIME, the kind of religious celebrations that we have conducted in the West have been filled with the spoken word and impossibly didactic. Almost all our religious observances are nothing but talk and consist of telling God what to do, as if He or She did not already know, and telling the people what to do, as if they were able or even willing to change. All of this is throwing the book at people, and telling them the Word, and I think we have had enough of it.

The history of religion in the West is nearly equivalent to the history of the failure of preaching. By and large, preaching is a kind of moral violence that excites people's sense of guilt, and there is no less creative sense than that. You cannot love and feel guilty at the same time, any more than you can be afraid and angry at the same time.

A Spiritual Experience

What seems to me to be lacking in our Western religious observances is some sort of ritual that gives us an opportunity for spiritual experience. By a spiritual experience I am referring to a transformation of the individual consciousness so that, in one way or another, the individual is able to realize his oneness with the eternal energy behind this universe, which some people call God and others prefer not to name or to conceive.

When Western people hear that an Asian practices meditation, they ask, "What do you meditate on?" But that question puzzles a Buddhist or a Hindu, because you do not meditate on anything, any more than you breathe on anything. You breathe, and in the same way, you meditate. The verb is in a way intransitive. Meditation is the act of allowing one's thoughts to cease.

Coming Into Touch with Reality

In the beginning of the *Yoga Sutra,* Patanjali described yoga — which means union — as spontaneously stopping the agitation of thinking. Thinking is talking to yourself, or figuring to yourself, and it is habitual for most of us. If I talk all the time, however, I do not hear what anyone else has to say. Equally, if I talk to myself all the time, I will not have anything to think about except thoughts.

There is no interval between thoughts during which I can come into touch with reality — that is to say, the world my thoughts represent, in the way words represent events, or money represents wealth. If I am never silent in my head, I will find myself living in a world of total abstraction divorced from reality altogether.

You may ask, "What is reality?" People have various theories about what it is, but it is important to remember that they are all theories. Those who believe that reality is material are projecting upon the world a certain philosophical theory about it, and those who say that it is mental, or spiritual, are doing likewise.

Reality itself is neither mental nor spiritual, nor any other concept that we can have of it; reality is simply the present moment.

You Cannot Meditate

Words are reality insofar as they are noises, but even that is saying too much. To meditate, you might think that you should attempt to suppress thought, but you don't do that because *you cannot meditate*. Let me repeat that emphatically: you cannot meditate. You, your ego image, can only chatter, because when it stops, it isn't there.

When you are not thinking, you have no ego,

because your ego is nothing more than a habitual concept. The thinker behind the thoughts and the feeler behind the feelings are only thoughts; each of these is an idea of some reference point to which all our experiences happen. That thought, however, cuts us off from what we experience and creates the illusion of a gap or gulf between the knower and the known.

This in turn is responsible for the feeling of alienation we have from the world, and as a result we suffer from conflict and hatred. The spirit of domination arises from that basic division that has been constructed in thought, and modern societies are typically obsessed with this highly destructive illusion.

When you come to an end of thought, you don't know how to meditate, and you don't know what to do with your mind, and nobody can tell you. But still, thinking comes to an end naturally, and you just watch.

You don't have to ask who watches because that question merely arises from the fact that in grammar every verb has to have a subject by rule — but that is not a rule of nature, it is a rule of grammar. In nature there can be watching without a separate watcher.

And So You Begin to Meditate

When you realize that you have come to your wit's end, you can begin meditation. Or meditation happens, and that happening is simply the watching of what is, of all the information conveyed to you by your exterior and interior senses, and even the thoughts that keep chattering on about it all.

You don't try to stop those thoughts, you just let them run as if they were birds twittering outside, and they will eventually become tired and stop.

But don't worry about whether they do or don't. Just simply watch whatever it is that you are feeling, thinking, or experiencing — that's it. Just watch it, and don't go out of your way to put any names on it. This is really what meditation is.

You are in meditation in an eternal present, and you are not expecting any result. You are not doing it to improve yourself, because you found that you can't. Your ego can't possibly improve you because it is what's in need of improvement, and your ego can't let go of itself because it is a complex of thoughts called "clinging to one's self." When it is finally understood that it is unable to achieve a transformation of consciousness, or the vivid sense of union of individual and cosmos, it just evaporates.

ONE OF THE EASIEST WAYS TO ENTER IN

One of the easiest ways to enter into the state of meditation, therefore, is listening to what is, and experiencing the qualities of sound.

Curiously enough, sound is a sense that bores us less

easily than sight. When you hear it, just listen to the random sounds that you know are going on in the room, or in the street. Listen as if you were listening to music, without trying to identify its source, to name it, or to put any label on it at all. Just enjoy whatever sound may be going on, whether it is outside or in the area where you are sitting. That is part of the ritual: just listen.

Letting Sound Happen through Us

We can go on from that listening to making sound ourselves while also listening to it. But instead of making sound, we will get the knack of letting it happen through us.

Once, a great choirmaster in England was rehearsing a choir in the presence of the archbishop of Canterbury, who was then William Temple, a great theologian. And this was a rather raw choir that didn't really know much about singing. The master gave them a hymn to sing that they knew very well, and to impress the archbishop they sang it with gusto, and it sounded forced and terrible.

Then the choirmaster asked them to sing a little-known hymn and had them go over it several times until everybody got the hang of it. "Now," he said, "I want you to sing this hymn again, but there's one very important thing: don't try to sing it. You mustn't try. You must think of the melody and let it sing itself." And they sang it very well.

Afterward he turned to the archbishop and said, "Your Grace, that's good theology, isn't it?" And it obviously was, since the archbishop told me the story.

MANTRA

In India we find the use of mantra — a mantra is what we would call a chant, where words and sounds are chanted not for their meaning but for their sound. Most mantras are not intended to be understood in a discursive and intellectual sense. Instead, you are asked only to go down into the sound, and the sound penetrates you. You are able to settle right to the bottom of it, because when you are listening to sound, and when you are letting sound hum through you, it is one of the most obvious manifestations of the energy of the universe.

It is commonly said in India that sound is Brahman, sound is God, and perhaps that is the original meaning of saying, "In the beginning was the Word." It did not mean that in the beginning was the chatter, or in the beginning was the commandment or the orders. It meant the vibration, the sound of the word.

So concentrate purely on the sound, and you will find some mantras that play in your ears are so simple that you will be able to join in with them effortlessly, and please do so quite freely.

It is a pity that the Roman Catholic Church, which

used to have a mantric service, is dropping it and putting the Mass in the vernacular, and not particularly good vernacular at that, as far as the English translation is concerned. It has begun to sound terribly intellectual, and often there is somebody standing by the altar with a microphone to explain what's going on, so that it is no longer possible to practice contemplative prayer at Mass. Instead you are hammered with information, with exultation, with edification all the time, and the Catholic Church should realize that in giving up Latin it has lost its magic.

Although we associate mantras with religion, they are not supposed to be understood, because religion is that which is past understanding. Understanding may lead up to it, but to express religion intellectually is to try to use the intellect for something it cannot do. It is comparable to picking up the telephone and dialing W-H-A-T I-S G-O-D, and expecting to get a useful answer. Although the telephone is very useful otherwise, you cannot find out the mystery of the universe through talk — only through awareness.

For that reason I have suggested that churches get rid of their pews, where everybody looks at the backs of each other's necks, and that they spread their floors with rugs and cushions, so that instead of a sermon they have a ritual in which people can approach an ineffable spiritual experience rather than being forced into a particular pattern of thinking.

In this spirit I have only given the slightest suggestion of how one uses the mantra, or the silence, for meditation. You all have your own way of doing things like that, so do it your own way. This technique is a vehicle, or a support for contemplation, and I suggest you simply sit quietly, and when you feel settled proceed into contemplation.

STILL THE MIND

Sit quietly and be with your breath, your mind, and all your feelings.

It doesn't matter whether you are sitting cross-legged or on your knees with your legs folded underneath you. The point is to settle into a posture that is stable and comfortable. You can cross your legs in front of you, or if you are limber you may wish to try the half-lotus or full-lotus position. You can sit on a cushion with your knees bent and legs on either side, or you can sit in a chair. The idea is to be comfortable and find a position that you can maintain effortlessly.

As you settle in, remember that although stillness is emphasized in meditation, this does not mean that you should hold still in a rigid way. Becoming still physically helps one to find stillness of mind, but if you need to move, get comfortable, so that you can settle even more deeply.

Keep your back upright and your head erect, but let

your arms relax. Rest the left palm in the right palm, and put your thumbs together as if you were holding an egg. Your hands should be positioned at your belly with your thumbs just below the navel.

If you are sitting cross-legged you may wish to rock back and forth for a moment to find your natural center. If you are sitting in a chair, plant your feet on the ground so that you are grounded.

Your mouth should be closed, the eyes lowered slightly.

When you have found a stable posture, allow your awareness to sink into your breath and to find the bottom of your breath. You are not trying to cultivate a particular kind of breath; just gently pay attention to your breathing. Allow the breath to come and go as it may.

That's all you need to do. Your body will become still, and your mind will naturally, at some point, become still as well.

That is the essential process of meditation.

If you wish, you can begin to hum when you feel comfortable with it. As your voice rises, begin to play with the sound.

The play of sound will eventually settle into a pattern, and a mantra will spontaneously form. Go with it, and in this moment you are experiencing ritual in its richest form.

About the Author

Alan Watts was born in England in 1915. Beginning at age sixteen, when he wrote essays for the journal of the Buddhist Lodge in London, he developed a reputation over the next forty years as a foremost interpreter of Eastern philosophies for the West, eventually developing an audience of millions who were enriched through his books, tape recordings, radio and television appearances, and public lectures. He became widely recognized for his Zen writings and for *The Book: On the Taboo Against Knowing Who You Are.*

In all, Watts wrote more than twenty-five books and recorded hundreds of lectures and seminars, all building toward a personal philosophy he shared with honesty and joy with his readers and listeners throughout the world. His overall works have presented a model of individuality and self-expression that can be matched by few philosophers.

Watts came to the United States in 1938, and earned a Master's Degree in Theology from Seabury-Western Theological Seminary. He was Episcopal Chaplain at Northwestern University during World War II, and held fellowships from Harvard University and the Bollingen Foundation. He became professor and dean of the American Academy of Asian Studies in San Francisco and lectured and traveled widely.

He died in 1973 at his home in northern California, survived by his second wife and seven children. A complete list of his books and tapes may be found at www.alanwatts.com.